A
NUCLEAR
POWER
PLANT

BUILDING
HISTORY
SERIES

A Nuclear Power Plant

by Marcia and Greg Lüsted

LUCENT BOOKS

An imprint of Thomson Gale, a part of The Thomson Corporation

San Diego • Detroit • New York • San Francisco • Cleveland
New Haven, Conn. • Waterville, Maine • London • Munich

For more information, contact
Lucent Books
27500 Drake Rd.
Farmington Hills, MI 48331-3535
Or you can visit our Internet site at http://www.gale.com

LIBRARY OF CONGRESS CATALOGING-IN-PUBLICATION DATA

Lüsted, Marcia, 1962–
  A nuclear power plant / by Marcia Lüsted and Greg Lüsted.
    p. cm. — (Building history)
Includes bibliographical references and index.
   ISBN: 1-59018-392-4 (hardcover: alk. paper)
  1. Nuclear engineering—Popular works. 2. Nuclear power plants—Popular works.
I. Lüsted, Greg, 1959– II. Title. III. Building history series.
  TK9146.L87 2004
  621.48'3—dc22

2004010681

Printed in the United States of America

Contents

FOREWORD

Throughout history, as civilizations have evolved and prospered, each has produced unique buildings and architectural styles. Combining the need for both utility and artistic expression, a society's buildings, particularly its large-scale public structures, often reflect the individual character traits that distinguish it from other societies. In a very real sense, then, buildings express a society's values and unique characteristics in tangible form. As scholar Anita Abramovitz comments in her book *People and Spaces*, "Our ways of living and thinking—our habits, needs, fear of enemies, aspirations, materialistic concerns, and religious beliefs—have influenced the kinds of spaces that we build and that later surround and include us."

That specific types and styles of structures constitute an outward expression of the spirit of an individual people or era can be seen in the diverse ways that various societies have built palaces, fortresses, tombs, churches, government buildings, sports arenas, public works, and other such monuments. The ancient Greeks, for instance, were a supremely rational people who originated Western philosophy and science, including the atomic theory and the realization that the earth is a sphere. Their public buildings, epitomized by Athens's magnificent Parthenon temple, were equally rational, emphasizing order, harmony, reason, and above all, restraint.

By contrast, the Romans, who conquered and absorbed the Greek lands, were a highly practical people preoccupied with acquiring and wielding power over others. The Romans greatly admired and readily copied elements of Greek architecture, but modified and adapted them to their own needs. "Roman genius was called into action by the enormous practical needs of a world empire," wrote historian Edith Hamilton. "Rome met them magnificently. Buildings tremendous, indomitable, amphitheaters where eighty thousand could watch a spectacle, baths where three thousand could bathe at the same time."

In medieval Europe, God heavily influenced and motivated the people, and religion permeated all aspects of society, molding people's worldviews and guiding their everyday actions. That spiritual mind-set is reflected in the most important medieval structure—the Gothic cathedral—which, in a sense, was a model of heavenly cities. As scholar Anne Fremantle so elegantly phrases it, the cathedrals were "harmonious elevations of stone and glass reaching up to heaven to seek and receive the light [of God]."

Our more secular modern age, in contrast, is driven by the realities of a global economy, advanced technology, and mass communications. Responding to the needs of international trade and the growth of cities housing millions of people, today's builders construct engineering marvels, among them towering skyscrapers of steel and glass, mammoth marine canals, and huge and elaborate rapid transit systems, all of which would have left their ancestors, even the Romans, awestruck.

In examining some of humanity's greatest edifices, Lucent Books' Building History series recognizes this close relationship between a society's historical character and its buildings. Each volume in the series begins with a historical sketch of the people who erected the edifice, exploring their major achievements as well as the beliefs, customs, and societal needs that dictated the variety, functions, and styles of their buildings. A detailed explanation of how the selected structure was conceived, designed, and built, to the extent that this information is known, makes up the majority of the volume.

Each volume in the Lucent Building History series also includes several special features that are useful tools for additional research. A chronology of important dates gives students an overview, at a glance, of the evolution and use of the structure described. Sidebars create a broader context by adding further details on some of the architects, engineers, and construction tools, materials, and methods that made each structure a reality, as well as the social, political, and/or religious leaders and movements that inspired its creation. Useful maps help the reader locate the nations, cities, streets, and individual structures mentioned in the text; and numerous diagrams and pictures illustrate tools and devices that bring to life various stages of construction. Finally, each volume contains two bibliographies, one for student research, the other listing works the author consulted in compiling the book.

Taken as a whole, these volumes, covering diverse ancient and modern structures, constitute not only a valuable research tool, but also a tribute to the human spirit, a fascinating exploration of the dreams, skills, ingenuity, and dogged determination of the great peoples who shaped history.

Important Dates in the Building of Nuclear Power Plants

1942
The first controlled nuclear reaction takes place at the University of Chicago.

1945
Atomic bombs are dropped on Hiroshima and Nagasaki, Japan.

1957
The first commercial nuclear reactor in the United States begins operation in Shippingport, Pennsylvania.

1961
The SL-1 reactor accident takes place in Idaho.

1973
The Arab oil embargo begins the U.S. energy crisis.

1976
The Clamshell Alliance, an antinuclear group, is formed in opposition to the Seabrook Nuclear Power Plant in New Hampshire.

1979
The Institute of Nuclear Power Operations (INPO) is created.

1942   **1960**   **1973**

1979
The worst nuclear power plant accident in the United States takes place at Three Mile Island in Pennsylvania.

1974
The Nuclear Regulatory Commission is created.

Nuclear power has had a controversial history.

1987
Congress chooses
Yucca Mountain
in Nevada as the
potential site for
a nuclear waste
storage facility.

2000
For the first time ever,
the Nuclear Regula-
tory Commission ap-
proves the renewal of
operating licenses for
commercial nuclear
power plants.

2003
The Northeast
blackout leaves
several states,
including cities
such as New
York, without
power.

1985
The National
Academy for
Nuclear Train-
ing is created.

1984	2000	2010

2001
Energy brownouts
take place in
California.

2010
Approximate date
for the opening
of the Yucca Mountain
waste repository.

1986
The world's worst
nuclear plant
accident takes place
at Chernobyl in the
Soviet Union.

2002
The Nuclear Power 2010
program is unveiled, with
the goal of building new
nuclear power plants in
the United States.

1984
Nuclear energy becomes the
second-largest source of electricity, second only to coal.

9

⌷ INTRODUCTION

The United States uses a tremendous amount of electricity every day, and the amount of electrical energy consumed by Americans has increased dramatically since the introduction of electricity over a hundred years ago. Electrical consumption has grown an average of 2 percent annually, but according to the Edison Electric Institute, consumption will increase by 51 percent between the years 2002 and 2025. More and more uses are continually being found for electricity, not just for the basic needs of household appliances, but also for other forms of technology, such as computers, DVD players, television, and entertainment systems, that have become a staple in most American households.

The electricity used in the United States is generated in several different ways: by using nuclear energy; by burning nonrenewable fossil fuels such as coal, oil, and natural gas; and by using renewable sources such as hydro (water), solar, geothermal, and wind power. Of these, nuclear energy accounts for 20 percent of the electricity used nationwide, and for some states it produces as much as 70 percent. Nuclear energy, however, is a misunderstood and often frightening idea to many people.

COMMON CONCERNS ABOUT NUCLEAR POWER

The biggest fear that many people have about nuclear energy concerns safety. Nuclear energy produces radiation, which is the energy and particles emitted from an unstable radioactive atom. These particles may interact with other atoms and create adverse effects. Although radiation is present in our food, air, soil, and water in small amounts, it is harmful to humans only in concentrated amounts. Many people fear that a nuclear power plant will accidentally emit dangerous levels of radiation into the atmosphere, affecting humans and the environment. Severe doses of radiation can lead to radiation sickness, which causes nausea, vomiting, loss of hair, and hemorrhaging. It eventually causes changes in human blood cells, leading to leukemia. Some scientists speculate that large amounts of non-naturally occurring radiation released to the environment may cause genetic mutations in plants and animals, and may also contaminate humans through ingestion of these contaminated food sources. Since the terrorist attacks on the World Trade

Center in New York City in September 2001, some people fear that nuclear power plants will be targets for terrorists; many people hold the common misconception that flying an airplane into a nuclear plant will result in a nuclear explosion. Nuclear energy also produces radioactive waste, which can be toxic to humans and must be stored securely within the plant itself or disposed of in a specially licensed waste disposal facility.

Despite all these potential hazards, nuclear power plants are extremely well regulated in order to address all of these issues and prevent incidents that would jeopardize public safety. The construction of a nuclear power plant involves painstaking attention to permits, licensing, and safety issues for this very reason.

POSITIVE ASPECTS OF NUCLEAR POWER

The positive aspects of nuclear power override many of the negative issues. As compared to fossil fuels, nuclear energy is clean, producing no emissions that are harmful to the environment, such as greenhouse gases, acid rain, or other air pollutants. Nuclear fuel in the form of uranium can be obtained within the United

When a uranium atom splits, it breaks up into atoms whose mass is less than that of the original uranium. The remaining mass is converted into enormous energy.

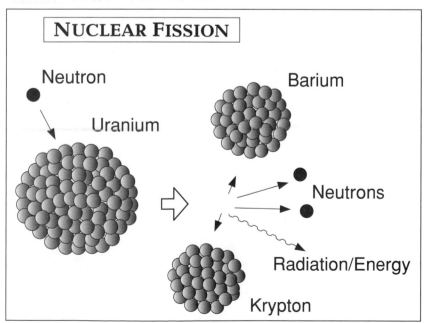

NUCLEAR FISSION

Neutron

Uranium

Barium

Neutrons

Radiation/Energy

Krypton

States, lessening the country's dependence on oil from foreign countries. Uranium is also much more economical than coal or oil, according to the Edison Electric Institute in its publication *Nuclear Power: Answers to Your Questions*:

> The fissioning of one uranium atom releases 50 million times more energy than the combustion of a single carbon atom common to all fossil fuels. Since a single small reactor fuel pellet [which is 3/8 of an inch in diameter and 5/8 of an inch in length, about the size of a pencil eraser] contains trillions upon trillions of atoms, an extremely large amount of energy is released. The amount of electricity that can be generated from three small fuel pellets would require about 3.5 tons of coal or 12 barrels of oil to generate.[1]

NUCLEAR ENERGY AND THE FUTURE

Currently there are more than one hundred nuclear power plants licensed to operate in the United States. Since the California energy crisis that caused widespread brownouts in 2001 and the Northeast blackout of August 2003, more attention is being paid to the amount of electricity being generated and how the current system will handle the ever-increasing needs of the country. As the World Energy Council stated in its publication *Energy for Tomorrow's World—Acting Now!*,

Children play in the shadow of a nuclear power plant in France. Nuclear power plants are highly regulated to ensure their safe operation.

AN EFFICIENT SOURCE OF POWER

Nuclear power plants produce as much as 20 percent of the electricity used in the United States. Worldwide, nuclear power accounts for 17 percent of the world's electricity.

According to the Energy Information Administration, a one-thousand-megawatt nuclear reactor operating at 80 percent capacity can produce 7 billion kilowatt hours of electricity in one year, enough to supply the electricity for 650,000 households. A kilowatt is a unit of energy equal to one thousand watts; the average lightbulb uses sixty to one hundred watts of power. If this power were generated by other fuel sources, it would require 11.6 million barrels of oil, or 3.5 million short tons of coal, or 70 billion cubic feet of natural gas.

It is a foregone conclusion that up to 2020 global reliance on fossil fuels and large hydro will remain strong, albeit with special emphasis on the role of natural gas and efficient cleaner fossil fuel systems. However, total reliance on these energy sources to satisfy the growing electricity demand of the world, especially in the context of two billion additional people who will need it by 2020, is not sustainable. The role of nuclear power therefore needs to be stabilised with the aim of possible future extensions. In parallel, efforts to develop intrinsically safe, affordable nuclear technology need to be encouraged.[2]

One of the possible solutions for increasing the energy supply will be the construction of new nuclear plants as older plants are decommissioned (retired), ensuring a continuing supply of nuclear energy for electricity. Nuclear plants are only licensed for a certain number of years, and when their useful time span ends, they cease operation and are dismantled.

Constructing a nuclear power plant is far from simple, however, involving many government regulations, environmental considerations, and community safety planning. The process takes many years. If we are to continue to meet the increasing demand for electricity in the United States by using more nuclear power, utilities and the government will need to streamline the planning and construction of new nuclear power plants and the creation of storage facilities for their radioactive waste.

THE BIRTH OF NUCLEAR POWER

When most people think about nuclear power, they think about its military uses, such as the nuclear warheads on missiles and the nuclear propulsion systems used in some of the navy's ships and submarines. However, nuclear power is also used in the production of electricity. In fact, nuclear energy provides a significant portion of the world's supply of electricity. The increasing use of nuclear power following the energy crisis of the 1970s, however, gave rise to several resistance groups that were concerned about the impact of nuclear energy on the environment and the safety of humanity.

DISCOVERING NUCLEAR POWER

Nuclear energy occurs on a microscopic level. All matter is made up of billions of tiny particles called atoms, and each atom has a nucleus, or center, consisting of protons and neutrons. In some types of atoms, such as uranium and plutonium atoms, this nucleus is unstable and breaks up, releasing the neutrons along with a great deal of heat. These neutrons then hit other atoms and force them to split, releasing even more neutrons and more heat. Nuclear power is created as a result of this process of splitting atoms, which is called fission.

In 1939, the United States experimented with nuclear fission. Because the process of fission releases an enormous amount of energy, it can set up a chain reaction of splitting in other nuclei. This reaction became the basis for creating the atomic bomb. In fact, the president at that time, Franklin Roosevelt, had already established the National Defense Research Committee to deal with the possibility of creating an atomic bomb. In 1942, the first demonstration reactor was built. By experimenting with nuclear fission in an enclosed area (within the reactor), scientists found that they could start and maintain a chain reaction of splitting nuclei, creating a controlled nuclear reaction. This research

Nuclear energy was first harnessed as a weapon. This missile built in 1957 was designed to carry a nuclear warhead.

culminated in the two atomic bombs that were dropped by U.S. army planes on Hiroshima and Nagasaki, Japan, in August 1945, in an effort to bring World War II in the Pacific to an end.

THE ATOMIC BOMBS

The two atomic bombs dropped on Japan in 1945 actually represented two different types of nuclear fission technology. They were the result of secret research carried out by the Manhattan Project, the largest civilian and military program of World War II. The Manhattan Project began in 1942 when several prominent American scientists believed that Germany had a six-month head start on developing its own atomic bomb. The Manhattan Project cost $2 billion and involved both military and civilian physicists and engineers. The bomb dropped on Nagasaki, nicknamed Fat Man after British prime minister Winston Churchill, used plutonium and had the equivalent of twenty-thousand tons of TNT, which is the conventional nonnuclear explosive used in bombs even today. The bomb dropped on Hiroshima was originally intended to be a gun-type bomb called

These models of Little Boy (left) and Fat Man (right), the atomic bombs dropped on Japan in 1945, are on display at a museum in Albuquerque, New Mexico.

Thin Man after President Franklin Roosevelt. Its design was not workable, however, so scientists constructed another bomb called Little Boy, which used uranium. Little Boy required an enormous amount of uranium, and scientists did not have enough processed uranium to test the bomb before it was used over Hiroshima. It had the equivalent power of fifteen thousand tons of TNT.

After the end of World War II, research focused on constructing bigger and better atomic bombs. Many of these bombs were mass-produced and stayed in America's nuclear arsenal until the late 1960s, when they were replaced by hydrogen bombs. The development of nuclear weapons resulted in an armament race between the United States and the Soviet Union; during the Cold War, from 1947 through 1991, each country tried to develop and stockpile more nuclear weapons than the other, resulting in the possibility of total mutual destruction. Planners on both sides used this threat of total destruction of both countries and possibly the entire planet as a deterrent to actual nuclear war, but the stockpiling of nuclear weapons continued until the dissolution of the Soviet Union began in 1991. Now both countries are downsizing the arsenals they built up during the Cold War.

OTHER USES FOR NUCLEAR POWER

The military had other uses for atomic energy besides these bombs. The military was interested in nuclear propulsion—using nuclear energy to power engines for ships, airplanes, submarines, and even automobiles and locomotives. The advantage of using nuclear propulsion for military transportation was that these vehicles would be able to travel long distances without frequent refueling stops. During the Cold War, the military was especially interested in developing an airplane that could fly overseas bombing runs and return to the United States without stopping. The U.S. Air Force developed a project for studying nuclear-powered aircraft, called Nuclear Energy for the Propulsion of Aircraft (NEPA). Unfortunately, atomic airplanes were found to be much too expensive to develop and maintain, so the project was discontinued. Nuclear-powered surface ships and submarines, however, were developed by the U.S. Navy and remain an important, cost-effective part of its fleet to this day.

The U.S. Army also built a floating nuclear power plant on a converted ship, the USS *Sturgis*. Instead of using the power

THE ATOMIC AIRPLANE

One of the most interesting nuclear energy projects that the United States experimented with involved nuclear propulsion—powering a ship, car, submarine, or airplane by nuclear energy instead of gasoline or diesel fuel. Scientists hoped that these experiments would result in a vehicle that would require less frequent refueling. Nuclear ships exist today, but other forms of nuclear-powered transportation were either scrapped on the drawing board or never made it past testing.

In 1946, the U.S. Air Force hoped to develop a nuclear-propelled bomber that could fly at least twelve thousand miles at a speed of 450 miles per hour without having to refuel. A nuclear-powered aircraft could potentially stay in the air for weeks at a time. The objective was to create a bomber aircraft that could fly to the Soviet Union to deliver a payload of atomic weapons and return without having to refuel, since at that time the United States feared nuclear war with the Soviets.

The air force converted a B-36 bomber, known as the nuclear test aircraft, to carry an operating nuclear reactor in its bomb bay. The plane was given a new nose section that used twelve tons of rubber and lead, as well as water-filled pockets, to shield the crew from the reactor. The designers even considered an aircraft with a detachable reactor module in front and the pilot cockpit in the tail section, making it possible to remove the reactor from the rest of the plane in an emergency. However, the converted bomber never made it past testing because of two major problems: the inability to find a material dense enough to shield the pilots from radiation but light enough to use on an aircraft, and the potential radiological danger if the plane should crash.

General Electric actually built two prototype engines for the nuclear-powered airplane. These still exist and can be seen in Arco, Idaho, at the EBR-1 testing facility, which is a national historic landmark.

for propulsion, this ship utilized its nuclear energy to generate electricity for shore-based installations. Stationed in Panama on Gatun Lake, the ship provided electrical power from its reactor via cables to the Canal Zone, a ten-mile strip of land surrounding the Panama Canal. It was the world's first floating nuclear power plant and produced energy from 1967 until 1976.

THE PEACEFUL ATOM

All of these military uses for nuclear energy, however, especially as it related to atomic weapons such as bombs and missiles, began to foster a worldwide movement for peaceful uses of atomic energy. As early as 1945, nuclear physicist Alvin Weinberg told the U.S. Senate's Special Committee on Atomic Energy, "Atomic power can cure as well as kill. It can fertilize and enrich a region as well as devastate it. It can widen man's horizons as well as force him back into the cave."[3]

In December 1953, the president of the United States, Dwight D. Eisenhower, appeared before the UN General Assembly and made a famous speech about the proliferation of atomic weapons and the future of the world:

> The United States . . . is instantly prepared to meet privately with other countries . . . to seek an acceptable solution to the atomic armament race which overshadows not only the peace, but the very life, of the world. The United States would seek more than the mere reduction or elimination of atomic materials for military purposes. It is not enough to take this weapon out of the hands of the soldier. It must be put into the hands of those who will know how to strip its military casing and adapt it to the arts of peace. . . . This greatest of destructive forces can be developed into a great boon, for the benefit of all mankind. Experts would be mobilized to apply atomic energy to the needs of agriculture, medicine, and other peaceful activities. A special purpose would be to provide abundant electrical energy in the power-starved areas of the world.
>
> The United States knows that peaceful power from atomic energy is no dream of the future. The capability, already proved, is here today.[4]

This speech became known as the peaceful atom speech, and it came to represent a new era in the use of atomic energy for civilian purposes. The media even tried to develop the idea of the atom as a positive, nonmilitary tool. In 1956 Walt Disney built an exhibit in his Tomorrowland theme park at Disneyland in California. Called Our Friend the Atom, the exhibit spotlighted atomic energy in cheerful, nondestructive applications, explaining the history of atomic research and the use of atomic

In 1956 an exhibit opened in Disneyland's Tomorrowland that promoted the use of nuclear power as a source of energy.

reactors to power the world. Disney published a children's book and made a companion film for his television show, all in the attempt to show the public, and especially children, that science could lead humans in peaceful directions.

The government began developing ideas for using atomic energy in everyday applications. It was seeking ways that nuclear explosions could be used for practical civilian purposes.

THE PLOWSHARE PROGRAM

One of the first attempts to find nonmilitary uses for nuclear energy was the Plowshare Program, established by the Atomic Energy Commission (AEC)—an international committee set up to provide a forum about nuclear energy—to research and develop peaceful, civilian uses of nuclear explosives. The program got its name from the biblical phrase about turning swords (weapons) into plowshares (a peaceful farming tool). The objective of the

Plowshare Program was to use nuclear explosives for large-scale excavations, quarrying, and underground engineering in order to build canals, harbors, railway passages, and underground storage reservoirs.

Between 1957 and 1962, the Plowshare Program considered various projects using nuclear explosives, such as Project Chariot, which would have excavated a harbor and ship-turning basin on the northwest coast of Alaska, and Project Carryall, which would have blasted a railroad pass in the Bristol Mountains of California. These projects were never carried out because they were too expensive and there was a serious problem of radioactive fallout, which was produced by nuclear explosions and could drift into too many high-population areas. The most ambitious Plowshare scheme was blasting a canal in Central America, but again the high cost and uncertain effects on public health canceled the project before it was ever begun.

OTHER USES OF NUCLEAR POWER

Nuclear, or atomic, energy is used for many different purposes. One of the biggest uses is in industry, where radioisotopes (natural or artificially made radioactive material) are used in tools, gauges, and imaging machines. Archaeologists also use natural radioactive materials in radiocarbon dating to determine the age of artifacts. Because all plants and animals on earth are made mostly of carbon, and a small percentage of this carbon is radioactive, scientists can measure the rate of decay of this radioactive carbon in a plant or bone sample and use it to date the age of the sample.

Nuclear energy is also used in health care. *Nuclear medicine* is the term used for the nuclear energy employed by hospitals in X-rays and in radiation therapy such as that used to treat cancer. Radiation is used in the food industry to irradiate food, a process that kills germs and keeps food fresh. Radioactive material is also used in the manufacture of home smoke detectors.

Nuclear power plays a large role in the space program. Nuclear science provides electrical power for radio equipment and sensors, as well as providing heat to protect delicate instruments from the intense cold of space. The nuclear power plant, however, continues to be the most visible and most advantageous use of nuclear power in the civilian world.

THE SHIPPINGPORT NUCLEAR POWER PLANT

Although the Plowshare Program failed to create nonmilitary uses for nuclear explosives, other uses for nuclear energy were being developed successfully. Great Britain and the Soviet Union, which were also making nuclear weapons, were the first countries to build industrial-scale nuclear power plants. The very first nuclear power plant was the Obninsk plant, a very small plant built in the Soviet Union in 1954. It generated only five megawatts of electricity (most plants in the world today generate more than a thousand megawatts) and was too small to have any commercial value, but it did serve as a prototype for later plants. In October 1956, the Calder Hall Nuclear Power Plant in northern England, the first nuclear reactor to provide electricity for both civilian and military uses, began distributing electricity. In 1957, the United States opened its first nuclear power plant in Shippingport, Pennsylvania, which began delivering electricity to Pittsburgh and the surrounding areas.

In October 1956 the world's first commercial nuclear power plant, England's Calder Hall Nuclear Power Plant, began operation.

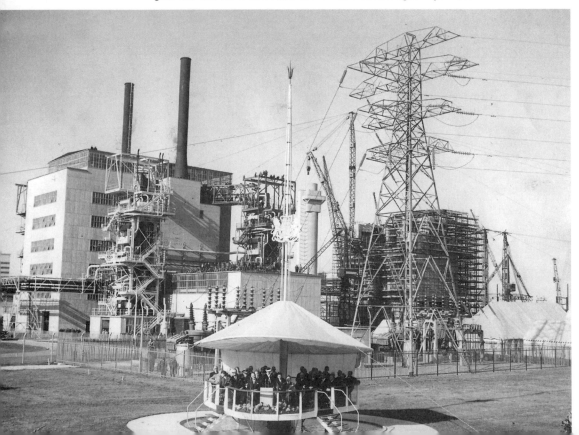

The reactor used in the Shippingport plant was originally intended for use in a nuclear-powered aircraft carrier, but the Eisenhower administration had vetoed the ship's construction. The administration argued that billions of dollars had already been spent on nuclear research for producing weapons and warships, but none for peaceful ventures. The British had already begun to build Calder Hall and the Russians were using the same technology, and the United States wanted to stay ahead of them in developing its own nuclear power plants. It was then proposed that the reactor could be used in a civilian power station, which would be in keeping with Eisenhower's desire to use the atom for applications that would benefit humankind.

The plant was approved by both the AEC and the Joint Committee on Atomic Energy (a U.S. government committee to oversee all atomic energy issues), and construction began shortly after. According to author Robert Martin, a very dramatic groundbreaking ceremony took place in September 1953:

> Ground was broken . . . with the wave of an "atomic wand" [containing a low level of radioactive material] from President Eisenhower [in Washington] over a Geiger counter that was used to send a signal over a telephone line to an unmanned bulldozer positioned to dig. On December 23, 1957, less than four and a half years after the construction contract had been signed, the Shippingport Nuclear Power Plant reached full power and was providing electricity to Pittsburgh.[5]

The actual building process was shrouded in secrecy, as most nuclear energy activities were at that time, due to fears that other countries would steal the United States' nuclear technology. At one time nuclear information was freely shared among the world's scientific community, but as soon as it became apparent that atomic research could lead to the development of a military weapon, the era of free exchange of information ended. Shippingport did serve as a valuable tool for developing, demonstrating, and testing nuclear designs and components, as well as for training nuclear personnel and for providing reliable information about the performance of a nuclear power reactor.

Calder Hall and Shippingport were just the beginning. As the world discovered the possibilities of producing electricity with nuclear energy, more and more plants were built. During

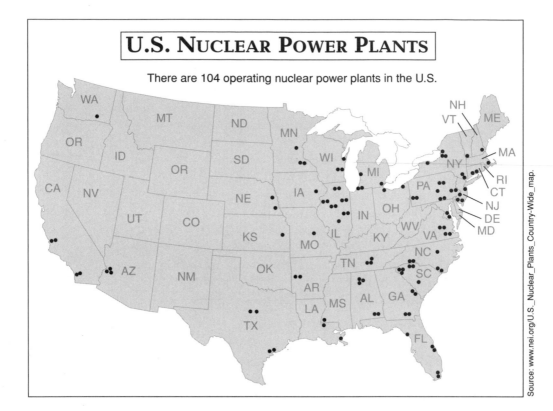

U.S. NUCLEAR POWER PLANTS

There are 104 operating nuclear power plants in the U.S.

the second half of the twentieth century, nuclear power plants were built at an increasing rate. The two leading vendors of nuclear plants, General Electric and Westinghouse, competed with each other to sell nuclear plants to utilities (companies that generate and transmit electricity to consumers) as a safe, reliable, and cost-effective alternative to fossil fuel plants. The vendors offered "turnkey" plants constructed for a fixed cost, meaning that the vendors would supply the entire plant and the utility would only have to "turn a key" to start operating it. These turnkey plants led to a boom in utilities purchasing nuclear power plants. From 1970 through the 1980s, almost one hundred new nuclear power plants began commercial operation in the United States.

THE ANTINUCLEAR MOVEMENT

As nuclear power plants proliferated, the public began to fear the environmental and health consequences of nuclear power. As early as 1940, scientists working in nuclear research grew

concerned about the enormous destructiveness of atomic bombs
and the fallout created by nuclear testing. Furthermore, the
bomb that was dropped on Hiroshima killed 150,000 people and
devastated the city. It also caused long-term health problems in
a portion of the population. In 1969, the Union of Concerned
Scientists was formed at the Massachusetts Institute of Technology to voice its members' concerns about the effects of nuclear technology on society, especially the destructive potential
of nuclear weapons and the safety issues that were still unre-
solved in the design of nuclear plants, especially their cooling
systems. This group still exists and is one of the most influential
critics of atomic energy today.

In the 1960s, civilians began to protest against the use of
nuclear energy to generate electricity, usually aiming their attacks at specific nuclear plants. By the early seventies, national
antinuclear groups were being formed, and some established

In the 1970s, Greenpeace began using its ship the Rainbow Warrior *to
disrupt nuclear testing around the world.*

environmental groups such as the Sierra Club added antinuclear activities to their agenda. These groups opposed nuclear energy because of the potential health and safety hazards from any radiation leaks or plant accidents, the cost overruns, and the problem of waste disposal. Friends of the Earth, an environmental group, began to protest nuclear energy in the early 1970s. Another group, Greenpeace, was established in Canada in 1971 to protest nuclear testing in Alaska. Its tactics included sailing a ship into the testing area in order to disrupt the tests. Greenpeace is now a worldwide organization that uses direct, nonviolent actions and publicity to achieve its goals.

THE FIRST ANTINUCLEAR DEMONSTRATIONS

Many nuclear power plants were directly affected by the protests of various antinuclear groups. The very first antinuclear campaign in the United States was sparked by the planned construction of the Meshoppen Nuclear Power Plant in the 1960s. Meshoppen, which was to be an experimental reactor in Pennsylvania, was supported by President John F. Kennedy. A scientist at the University of Pittsburgh, however, presented research that suggested a rise in deaths from cancer due to radiation in the vicinity of nuclear plants. Although other scientists later examined his conclusions and thought that the risk had been exaggerated, the fear of radiation was strong enough that a delegation of concerned local citizens, including many Quakers in what was the first instance of a religious group taking an antinuclear stance, testified before a Senate committee in an attempt to block construction. The project was resited to the Clinch River in Tennessee, where there was less opposition to its construction.

Antinuclear demonstrations were not just a U.S. occurrence. In 1975, the citizens of Whyl, a small village in West Germany, launched a major protest against the construction of a nuclear power station in their area. Their initial concern was that the humidity from the plant's cooling towers (the structures where hot water from the plant is circulated in order to cool it down for reuse) would have a negative effect on the nearby vineyards, where most of the people of Whyl made their living growing grapes. Soon the issue escalated into a protest over reactor safety. According to Stephen E. Atkins in his book *A Historical Encyclopedia of Atomic Energy*,

Whyl's 300 citizens started the protest by occupying the construction site, sitting down in front of bulldozers and halting work. German police attempted to drive off the demonstrators without much success. Once the news was exposed on the national media, supporters flocked to Whyl. It has been estimated that there were over 20,000 demonstrators taking part, and the site was occupied for a year. Moreover, the participants began a study program to educate and recruit antinuclear activists.[6]

Finally a lawsuit was brought against this organized opposition, but ultimately the utility canceled its plans and the reactor was never built. The success of the Whyl demonstration became a model for other protests all over the world.

THE CLAMSHELL ALLIANCE

One of the most famous antinuclear groups in the United States was formed exclusively to protest the construction of a nuclear plant in New Hampshire. The Clamshell Alliance was formed in July 1976 in Rye, New Hampshire, as a coalition opposing

In 1978 a large group of protesters known as the Clamshell Alliance demonstrates against the construction of the Seabrook Nuclear Power Plant in New Hampshire.

Protesters hold a candlelight vigil on the first anniversary of the 1979 nuclear accident at the Three Mile Island Nuclear Power Plant.

the Seabrook Nuclear Power Plant. The Clamshell Alliance got its name from the clam beds in the Seabrook area, which fishermen feared would be destroyed by the location of the nuclear plant and the thermal pollution that might result from the plant discharging warm water into the ocean. This group practiced civil disobedience, using nonviolent techniques to protest the plant, culminating in a huge demonstration and sit-in in 1977 that led to the arrest of over fourteen hundred people for trespassing on the construction site.

Because the media paid so much attention to the Clamshell Alliance, other groups all over the country began to imitate its tactics to protest the construction of nuclear power plants. These groups included the Abalone Alliance in California, the Oystershell Alliance in Louisiana, the Crabshell Alliance in Washington State, the Sunflower Alliance in Kansas, and the Palmetto Alliance in South Carolina.

The antinuclear movement in America gained even more momentum after the Three Mile Island accident in Harrisburg, Pennsylvania, in 1979, when a small amount of radiation was inadvertently released into the atmosphere, and the Chernobyl accident in the Soviet Union (now Russia) in 1986, when the plant suffered a major meltdown and fire, releasing radiation into the environment. After these events, the construction of nuclear power plants was drastically cut back and the United States seemed to have abandoned the idea of depending on nuclear power as a basis for future energy production.

THE ENERGY CRISIS OF THE 1970S

Despite the vocal antinuclear groups, however, the 1970s were the peak years of nuclear power plant construction. This was mostly due to the energy crisis that affected the United States during this time.

Oil shortages during the 1970s resulted in scenes like this at gas stations across the United States. The shortage also made nuclear power an attractive option.

Before 1973, Americans were confident that their energy demands would always be met, and they did not really worry about the supply of oil or sharp price increases. But energy consumption increased by 50 percent in the 1970s, and U.S. oil production could no longer keep pace with the demand, leading to a reliance on foreign oil sources. In 1973, Americans suddenly faced electricity brownouts (when there was power available but not enough to meet the demand) and rapidly rising prices for fuel. Price controls (government attempts to set a price limit for energy products such as oil and gasoline) and systems for distributing oil fairly according to need did not work, and then in October 1973, the Organization of Petroleum Exporting Countries (OPEC) in the Middle East restricted the amount of oil being sold to the United States. This created even greater shortages of oil and gasoline and elevated prices to a level most consumers could not comprehend. Customers had to line up at gas stations and frequently found that those stations had run out of fuel completely. Consumers began to purchase smaller, more fuel-efficient cars and paid more attention to their electrical consumption and the efficiency of their appliances.

This shortage of oil forced the government to take steps to increase American oil production, as well as exploring other means for generating electricity, such as nuclear power. During this time nuclear energy technologies were expanded and different types of plants were constructed, until the nuclear industry was able to develop plants that were best able to meet the energy needs of the United States.

INSIDE A NUCLEAR POWER PLANT

The types of nuclear power plants in use in the United States today are a result of the experimentation and growth of the 1970s, brought on by the energy crisis and utilities having the money to spend on new technologies and power plants. The number of U.S. nuclear plants increased from 15 to 74 reactors during this time, and currently there are 104 operating plants, producing 20 percent of the nation's electricity.

Although the nuclear power plants in the United States are not all exactly alike, these plants share the same basic buildings and equipment, such as the cooling towers, the containment building, the turbine building, and the fuel storage building. These buildings may be arranged differently at every plant, but they all are necessary for the safe, efficient operation of the nuclear reactor, which is the heart of the plant.

A NUCLEAR PLANT SITE

The most familiar component of a nuclear plant site, and the structures that most people identify with a nuclear plant, are the cooling towers. In most power plants, these cooling towers are large, concrete, hourglass-shaped towers used to remove heat from the water that circulates through the equipment in the turbine building. Above the cooling tower, a cloud of warm water vapor rises into the air. This kind of cooling tower utilizes natural draft: The warm water heats the air and causes it to rise out of the top of the cooling tower. Plants that do not have this kind of cooling tower may use a lower-profile cooling system that utilizes fans to create a draft inside a row of smaller cooling towers.

Another recognizable building at a nuclear power plant is the containment building, which holds the nuclear reactor. Depending on the type of nuclear plant, the containment building may be either a square, tall structure or the more distinctive,

The giant, hourglass-shaped cooling towers are the most recognizable feature of most nuclear power plants.

dome-topped building that many people associate with nuclear plants. The containment building is made of concrete and steel and has to be tall enough to accommodate the cranes that are used inside for moving heavy machinery or fuel.

Another building found at a nuclear power plant is the turbine building, which is usually shorter and longer than the containment building. It contains the steam turbines and generator that convert heat from the nuclear reactor into electricity.

The power plant also contains a number of other buildings and structures that are relatively nondescript but perform important functions. These include the waste process building for handling wastes, the fuel storage building, a building that houses a diesel generator, and buildings for handling intake water from nearby water sources. The plant site will also include administrative and service buildings for offices, training, and fire prevention activities.

The heart of any nuclear power plant is not visible from the exterior of the plant. This is the nuclear reactor itself, housed in a protective reactor vessel that is further protected inside the containment building. The way in which the reactor produces electricity depends on the type of plant.

TYPES OF NUCLEAR POWER PLANTS

The nuclear power plants in the United States are light water reactors, or LWRs. The LWR plant is very similar to a conventional fossil-fuel plant except that it uses nuclear fuel instead of coal or oil to create the steam for the electrical generator. Stephen E. Atkins describes LWRs in his book *Historical Encyclopedia of Atomic Energy:*

> The standard design for most American nuclear reactors was the light water reactor (LWR). This reactor uses enriched uranium as fuel and regular water as a coolant. High-pressure water passes around the reactor, which heats the water before it is transferred to a steam generator. It was designed in the late 1940s and became popular because of the simplicity of its design.[7]

LWRs are broken down into two different types: the boiling water reactor (BWR) and the pressurized water reactor (PWR). The BWR and the PWR operate in a similar way and utilize the same nuclear fuel cycle and systems for containment, cooling, waste processing, and power generation. However, these two types of plants differ in the way that cooling water is used and steam is produced.

In a BWR, the water is pumped in a closed cycle, which means that the water is constantly reused and never leaves the system. The heat generated by the nuclear reactor is transferred to the water, which flows around the nuclear fuel. The water boils, and a mixture of steam and water flows to the top of the nuclear reactor. Once the steam and water reach the top, they are separated and the steam is passed to the turbine generator, where the turbine converts the steam energy into rotational energy to turn the generator and create electricity. This steam has a temperature of 545 degrees Fahrenheit. The steam exhaust from the turbine is condensed back into water and returned to the reactor. The energy supplied to the water by the hot fuel is transferred directly to the turbine as steam, and so the BWR is called a direct cycle system.

The other type of LWR is the pressurized water reactor, or PWR. In a PWR, there are two coolant loop systems for transferring energy from the reactor to the turbine. The primary loop contains water that is pumped through the nuclear core and a heat exchanger, called a steam generator, and then back to the core. Another, secondary loop contains water that is pumped through the other side of the steam generator, producing steam that goes to the turbine. The steam generator essentially exchanges the heat from one coolant loop into the other. The exhaust steam from the turbine is condensed back into water and

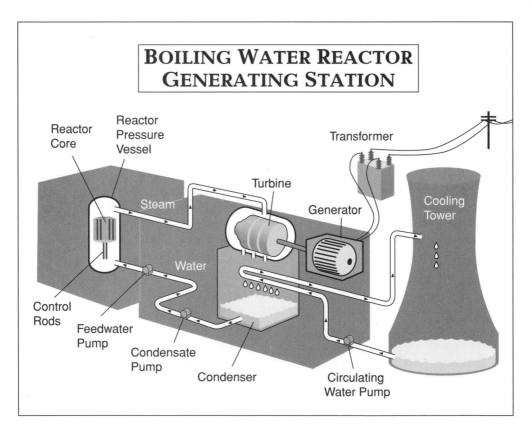

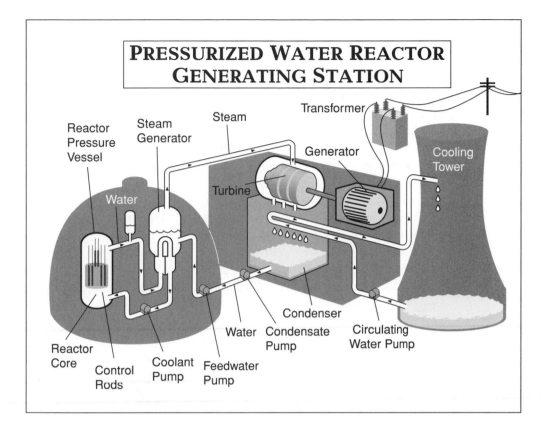

PRESSURIZED WATER REACTOR GENERATING STATION

travels back in the second loop through the steam generator in a continuous cycle.

THE BREEDER REACTOR

Other types of reactors have been or are still being considered for use in this country. A few were even constructed and used, but they were not considered practical, safe, or cost-effective for permanent use.

The breeder reactor was developed to use plutonium fuel to produce energy and to also produce more plutonium than it used. Plutonium is a human-made element manufactured from uranium. The excess plutonium could then be used to fuel other breeder reactors, in something like a recycling process. Breeder reactors were especially attractive in the late 1940s and the 1950s when uranium was in short supply. Breeder reactors were thought to be the reactors of the future because they would be able to produce an inexhaustible supply of energy at a relatively low cost.

In 1966, an experimental breeder reactor plant called Fermi I was constructed on the shores of Lake Erie outside of Detroit, Michigan. Breeder reactors were considered the most hazardous of all reactors because they used sodium for coolant, even though sodium was less stable than using water and presented a greater risk for cooling problems. Fermi I generated considerable protests and was even challenged in the Supreme Court, but its construction was allowed and it began producing electricity in early 1966. In October 1966, however, the plant's core suffered a partial meltdown after a piece of metal became dislodged in the reactor and partially blocked the flow of coolant. The reactor was shut down and was decommissioned in 1970 without ever having operated economically.

Breeder reactors are difficult to build and maintain because they require a great deal of equipment and constant maintenance. In breeder reactors the nuclear reaction takes place at a very high speed because of the different method used for creating nuclear fission, so any flaw in the cooling system can have catastrophic results. In 1978, one of Russia's breeder reactors was the site of a narrowly averted accident. Located in Beloyarsk, in what was then the Soviet Union, the plant had two conventional reactors and a new, fast breeder reactor. According to Stephen E. Atkins in the *Historical Encyclopedia of Atomic Energy*,

> An explosion in the machine hall caused the roof to fall into the building, making cables short out. In case of fire, the operators were to shut down both [conventional] reactors, but because the temperature outside was –60 degrees Centigrade [–76 degrees Fahrenheit] the reactor cooling systems would freeze and allow the reactor cores to overheat. Fearing a double meltdown, the operators decided to shut down only one reactor. Fire crews had arrived, but it looked like the situation was out of control with the fire raging. As the fire reached the computer room, the firefighters gained control . . . and the meltdowns were avoided. While no radioactivity escaped from the reactors, the accident was a close call for a major disaster.[8]

The United States no longer uses breeder reactors. The only countries still utilizing breeder reactor technology at this time are India, France, Japan, and Russia.

EXPERIMENTAL NUCLEAR REACTORS

There is another type of nuclear power plant, which South Africa is currently experimenting with. It is called a pebble-bed reactor, and it operates in much the same way as the existing nuclear reactors with one major difference. The uranium fuel is encased in graphite "pebbles" the size of billiard balls, which cannot get hot enough to melt. This prevents the kind of nuclear accident that people fear might occur in conventional plants, where a loss of coolant to the reactor would cause a meltdown of the uranium fuel in the plant's reactor core. These pebbles are also less likely than fuel rods to be damaged during long-term storage.

Scientists continue to experiment in an effort to create newer nuclear reactor technologies that will be safer and create less waste than existing systems. These experimental reactors include the Advanced Boiling Water Reactor, the Advanced

This experimental breeder reactor was built in Idaho in the 1990s. Breeder reactors create power as well as extra plutonium for use in new reactors.

POWER PLANT DIVERS

One of the most surprising professions associated with a nuclear power plant is professional scuba diving. Divers are used in nuclear plants in many construction, maintenance, and refueling operations in both nonradioactive and contaminated environments. They inspect and repair piping systems and clean and repair trash racks (which collect debris from ocean or lake water before it enters the plant). They also inspect tanks and vats and repair pump systems. Within contaminated water in the nuclear plant itself, they enter the spent fuel pool to rearrange the racks of spent fuel and do video inspections of the reactor cavity. Divers also perform metal welding and cutting, as well as concrete repair.

Divers are closely monitored for radiation exposure. They wear diving suits and helmets that protect them from the radiologically contaminated water, though the water itself is a shield against radiation. Divers wear electronic radiation monitoring devices on different parts of their bodies, so they can be monitored on the surface by another worker who will know exactly how much radiation that diver is receiving. If the amount of radiation is too high, the diver will be removed from the area.

Any diving equipment used for nuclear jobs remains on the site and becomes the property of the utility, because the utility is licensed to safely store contaminated equipment. Some divers leave their equipment at one site until it is needed at their next job at another site. Then it can be shipped with the proper radiological controls. This way, the divers do not need to be licensed to store their own radioactive materials. Divers purchase equipment of high quality because it cannot be sent back to the manufacturer for repair once it has been contaminated.

Liquid Metal Reactor, the Integrated Fast Reactor, and the Modular High Temperature Gas Cooled Reactor. These experimental types of reactors incorporate advantages such as fuel recycling, less frequent refueling outages, or the use of reactor coolants such as liquid metal or gas.

Until these experimental reactors prove successful, however, the United States will continue to use LWRs. To understand how LWRs have been constructed, it is helpful to understand how a nuclear power plant produces electricity. This process begins with the nuclear fuel cycle, which provides the raw materials for nuclear energy. All nuclear reactors share this same fuel cycle.

THE NUCLEAR FUEL CYCLE

The heart of a nuclear power plant is the nuclear reactor itself, but without nuclear fuel to create the reaction, the reactor is merely a piece of machinery. The nuclear fuel cycle is the process of mining uranium and processing it into nuclear fuel. Ninety-five percent of the uranium mined in the United States is found in New Mexico, Wyoming, Utah, Nebraska, Arizona, Texas, Washington, and Colorado.

The first nuclear reactors in America used ore that was mined in Canada, north of the Arctic Circle. This mine, called the Eldorado Mine, was discovered in 1930. The mine was in such a remote location—sixteen hundred miles from the nearest railroad—that the uranium ore it produced could be transported only by water. This meant that the mine could operate only for three months out of the year, when the nearby rivers and lakes were unfrozen. The United States had such a tremendous demand for uranium for its experimental reactors and weapons that it was able to contract with the Eldorado Mine to reserve its entire production. The mine continued to produce uranium ore until 1960, when it finally gave out. By then, the United States had discovered its own sources of uranium in the western area of the country.

Uranium is mined in open pits or underground mines, and the uranium content of the mined ore is often as low as 0.1 or 0.2 percent, so tremendous amounts of ore must be mined to get at the uranium. The raw uranium ore is then transported to a mill, usually located near the mine to limit shipping distance. A uranium mill is basically a chemical plant where the ore is crushed and sulfuric acid is used to extract the uranium from the crushed ore, leaving any extra materials behind. This process creates a powder called yellowcake, named for its rough texture and yellow color, although yellowcake actually varies in color from yellow to orange to dark green, depending on the temperature at which it was dried. Yellowcake is packed in casks and shipped to a government-owned processing plant, where it is purified for use in reactors. The government owns the processing plant in order to ensure the quality of the product and regulate the supply of uranium and its availability for power plants, particularly since

This open-pit uranium mine is located in New Mexico. Tons of ore are needed to produce a small amount of usable uranium.

uranium was in limited supply in the 1940s and 1950s. Because uranium is also used in nuclear weapons, it is controlled by the government for that reason as well.

The government-owned conversion plant processes the uranium by enriching it, or increasing the fuel concentration. Certain types of reactors require certain concentrations of the uranium, and the electric utility that owns the power plant pays the government a service charge for this enrichment operation.

The next step in the fuel cycle is fuel preparation, in which the fuel is shaped into pellets the size of a pencil eraser. The pellets are then arranged end to end and sealed in long metal tubes known as cladding or fuel rods. Groups of these fuel rods are then bundled together to form the fuel assemblies that will be used in the nuclear reactor. These assemblies are then packed and shipped to nuclear plants to be stored until they are placed inside the reactor core.

Fuel and Reactor Control

Once the power plant has its supply of fuel, the first step has been taken toward producing power. The next step of the process is the system for using the fuel within the reactor.

The fuel assemblies are arranged in a specific pattern according to the type of power plant they will be used in. A BWR usually has four fuel bundles consisting of 64 rods in an 8-by-8 pattern. In the center of the fuel assembly is a cross-shaped cavity for the control rod. The control rod absorbs the neutrons thus regulating the fission process. A PWR fuel assembly usually requires a larger number of fuel rods. The fuel assembly is a single bundle of 225 rods arranged in a 15-by-15 pattern. A control rod mechanism in the center of the bundle consists of several smaller tube-shaped control rods. However, the arrangement of the fuel rods in each nuclear plant varies somewhat depending on its size and generation capacity.

Gloved workers prepare uranium for use in fuel rods. The number of rods needed for energy production depends on the type of reactor.

The control rods within each fuel assembly function much like the controls in a car, accelerating the neutron fission process when they are withdrawn and acting like a brake on the fission process when they are inserted. In a BWR, the control rods are driven from the bottom of the reactor upward, but in a PWR the control rods are driven downward from the top of the reactor.

The fuel rod assemblies for a nuclear power plant are contained within the reactor pressure vessel, which is made out of thick steel (from six to eight and a half inches in thickness). The steel is then lined with stainless steel to reduce corrosion. In a PWR, this reactor vessel is located within the characteristic concrete dome-shaped building. A BWR, however, has its reactor vessel within a smaller containment, which is inside a rectangular building. These power plants are less identifiable as nuclear plants to the casual observer.

COOLING SYSTEMS

BWR and PWR plants, as previously mentioned, use coolant water in different ways, with the BWR recirculating the same water in a closed loop and the PWR operating with multiple closed recirculating loops that exchange heat from one to the other. Each cooling system requires pumps to recirculate the coolant water. A PWR also requires a steam generator to transfer heat from the primary coolant to the secondary loop, turning its water into steam to drive the turbine and produce electricity. As its name implies, a BWR makes its steam inside the pressure vessel, which is then used by the turbine directly.

There is also a separate water system for condensing the steam used by the turbine back into water so it can be sent back to the reactor for reuse. This circulating water is usually drawn from a nearby source such as a river, lake, or ocean. The condenser, which is part of the cooling system, is located at the turbine exhaust and contains a large number of tubes through which this cool external water is circulated. As the water passes through the tubes, it absorbs heat from the steam, causing the steam itself to turn to water. This water inside the tubes is now hot and must be piped to the cooling tower where its temperature drops as heat is given up to the atmosphere. Once the temperature is reduced, the water is reused and circulated through the condenser.

FINDING A CONTRACTOR

When a utility decides to construct a nuclear power plant, it needs to hire a contractor to oversee the entire project. Construction on the scale of a power plant requires someone more experienced than a local city contractor who may have built small factories or industrial buildings. Nuclear power plants need to be constructed by experienced companies that are familiar with the increasingly complex regulations and codes that must be followed during every step of construction. The company may hire craftsmen, such as pipe-fitters or electricians, from the local area, but a company completely familiar with the process manages the overall project and is also responsible for making sure that the workers are trained to the proper standards.

Many large construction companies specialize in projects such as power plants. Once a utility has determined the size, power capacity, and design of the future power plant, it will invite companies to bid on the project. Usually the company with the lowest bid will be hired to do the job.

WASTE DISPOSAL

Another element common to all nuclear plants is the disposal of radioactive waste. Radioactive waste can be in the form of liquids or solids. The quantity of each kind of waste varies depending on the type of plant. In its publication *Nuclear Power: Answers to Your Questions*, the Edison Electric Institute describes the spent fuel, which is the greatest disposal issue faced by nuclear power plants:

> Spent nuclear fuel is considerably more radioactive than new fuel. A person can handle new fuel pellets of uranium oxide without danger. In contrast, spent fuel is dangerously radioactive, although much of the radioactivity dissipates quickly—some 98 percent within six months. Forty to fifty years after spent fuel is removed from the reactor, its radioactivity has decreased by a factor of 100. A very small percentage of nuclear wastes remain radioactive for thousands of years.[9]

Nuclear plants have on-site radioactive waste treatment systems to minimize the amount of radioactive waste released to the environment. However, some plants are running out of space to store their waste and are being forced to construct on-site storage casks until the nuclear waste can be shipped to a permanent storage facility.

Solid wastes, such as contaminated filters, clothing, tools, rags, and spent reactor parts, are put into containers and buried at a government-licensed radioactive-waste landfill. Sometimes the solid waste is incinerated at a licensed radioactive incinera-

A technician at a nuclear waste storage facility checks radiation levels at the site. Such facilities are government controlled.

tion facility and just the resulting radioactive ashes are buried. Metals may be melted down into large blocks before disposal.

Used fuel bundles are the biggest disposal challenge for a nuclear power plant. Most fuel bundles are removed from the reactor when spent and placed in a spent fuel pool on-site, a specially constructed concrete water pool, lined with welded stainless steel, that acts as a radiation shield as well as a means of removing the decay heat from the spent fuel. The size of the pool depends on the size of the fuel rods used in that particular plant. These pools were originally intended to be large enough to hold enough spent fuel to last the life of the plant. Because power plants have a finite amount of storage space in their spent fuel pools, and because plants are being licensed for longer operating periods than they were originally built for, storage of the used fuel bundles is one of the issues that limit the continued operation of a nuclear plant. The government is currently constructing a permanent waste storage site for high-level radioactive waste at Yucca Mountain in Nevada. The United States currently does not reprocess any of its spent nuclear fuel, although that process would create more fresh fuel for the reactors and result in less waste that requires disposal.

With all the systems involved in the generation and maintenance of a nuclear power plant, it is not easy for a utility to construct and operate one. The licensing and regulation process is long and complicated, and it must be completed before construction can even begin. The most difficult part of the process involves finding the site where the plant will be built.

Finding a Site for a Nuclear Power Plant

Of all the challenges involved in constructing a new nuclear power plant, the one that is most vital to its future safe operation is finding and evaluating a site for the plant. When a utility company decides to build a new nuclear power plant, it cannot simply place the plant on whatever piece of land it has and begin construction immediately. Building a new nuclear power plant is a long and difficult undertaking. There are many permits to obtain and procedures that must be followed in a complicated process that begins with the U.S. Nuclear Regulatory Commission, known as the NRC.

A control room operator in a nuclear power plant runs tests with the help of a hefty operations manual. Safety is a top priority at all nuclear power plants.

THE NUCLEAR REGULATORY COMMISSION

The NRC is the regulator of nuclear power in the United States. It was established as a result of the Energy Reorganization Act of 1974. Before that, one agency, the Atomic Energy Commission (AEC), had been responsible for both the development and production of nuclear weapons, and the development and safety regulation of all civilian (nonmilitary) uses of nuclear power. The act of 1974 gave the Department of Energy the responsibility for nuclear weapons and created the NRC for the regulation of civilian nuclear power.

Both the AEC and the NRC adopted a policy of industry self-regulation, where the responsibility for safety in nuclear plants was left up to the operators of those nuclear facilities. The nuclear plant itself was responsible for implementing safety training programs and procedures, as well as operating procedures for everyday running of the plant. It took a near meltdown at a nuclear plant to make the NRC realize that it needed to be more closely involved in all the construction and safety aspects of nuclear power plants.

THE BROWN'S FERRY INCIDENT

The fire that occurred at the Brown's Ferry Nuclear Station near Decatur, Alabama, on March 22, 1975, revealed that the safety regulations at nuclear plants were inadequate. The Brown's Ferry plant had two reactors, which were running at full capacity. At the time, two electricians were in the cable spreading room. This room houses the electrical cables that control the two reactors, and since these cables penetrate into the reactor containment building itself, workers try to minimize air leaks to keep the containment building sealed as tightly as possible. These electricians were finding and sealing air leaks, using a candle flame to see if the leaks had been successfully plugged, since an air leak would make the flame flicker.

The electricians found a leak and were attempting to seal it when a fire started. According to one of the electricians, as quoted in an NRC report,

> We found a 2 x 4 inch opening in a penetration window in a tray with three or four cables going through it. The candle flame was pulled out horizontal showing a strong draft. D [the other electrician] tore off two pieces of foam

sheet for packing into the hole. I rechecked the hole with the candle. The draft sucked the flame into the hole and ignited the foam, which started to smoulder and glow. D handed me his flashlight with which I tried to knock out the fire. This did not work and then I tried to smother the fire with rags stuffed in the hole. This also did not work and we removed the rags. Someone passed me a CO_2 extinguisher with a horn which blew right through the hole without putting out the fire, which had gotten back into the wall. I then used a dry chemical extinguisher, and then another, neither of which put out the fire.[10]

The fire started by the electricians burned out of control for over seven hours, destroying many of the plant's cables, including most of those that controlled the safety systems. The two reactors were finally shut down, narrowly avoiding damage to the nuclear fuel.

The Brown's Ferry incident pointed out that interpretation of safety systems rules and regulations and the development of related training and procedures varied widely from plant to plant. There were too many possibilities for major accidents to occur unless the NRC started to take a more active part in establishing and monitoring safety in all nuclear plants.

Today, the NRC is responsible for regulating commercial nuclear reactors as well as those that are used for testing and training; monitoring the uses of nuclear materials in medical, industrial, and academic settings; overseeing the transportation, storage, and disposal of nuclear waste; and decommissioning nuclear facilities when they are removed from service. According to the NRC, "The NRC's mission is to regulate the Nation's civilian use of byproduct, source, and special nuclear materials to ensure adequate protection of public health and safety, to promote the common defense and security, and to protect the environment."[11]

When a utility decides to construct a nuclear power plant, the NRC has a very big role in how a site for the plant is chosen, especially since its mission involves public health and safety and preserving the environment. Before any work can be done, the utility must contact the NRC, undergo a long permit and planning process, and choose a site according to specific, established NRC guidelines.

Nuclear power plant workers in protective suits inspect and replace components as part of routine maintenance procedures established by the NRC.

GEOLOGY AND SEISMOLOGY

A nuclear plant cannot be built just anywhere. Because of the extreme importance of keeping the plant safe and also safeguarding the surrounding areas, the utility company must consider many factors before building the plant and bringing it up to power to produce electricity.

The most important consideration in siting a nuclear plant is the geology and seismology (the potential for earthquakes) of the area. The area being considered for a new plant must be carefully studied for potential earthquakes, landslides, and sudden shifting of soil, which might result in ground collapse. These are known as design-basis phenomena. Ideally, the plant should be constructed in an area with a minimal possibility of any of these events, and if there is a possibility, then the plant must be carefully planned and built so as to withstand these events.

For example, when the Diablo Canyon Nuclear Power Plant was being planned in coastal California near San Luis Obispo, the biggest concern for both the utility company constructing the plant and the public was that an earthquake fault called the Hosgri Fault was located just two miles from the potential plant site. The NRC therefore required the utility to include special seismic designs in the plant's blueprints, such as using special steel, heavy piping, and strong foundations and walls specially engineered to withstand the additional movement and stress of

The Diablo Canyon Nuclear Power Plant in central California was specially designed to withstand the stresses of earthquakes.

DIABLO CANYON'S EARTHQUAKE

On December 22, 2003, California experienced an earthquake of 6.5 magnitude on the Richter scale, about thirty-five miles north of the Diablo Canyon Nuclear Power Plant. Although the plant is located near the Hosgri Fault, geologists believe that this quake occurred on a different fault.

After the earthquake was felt by the operators in the plant's control room and registered on the plant's seismic monitors, the plant declared an Unusual Event, which is the lowest emergency classification used by a power plant. An Unusual Event does not require any emergency action by the government or general public. The plant did not shut down and continued to operate normally.

Shortly after the earthquake, California senator Barbara Boxer called for the NRC to perform an emergency inspection of the plant, especially its foundations and structures, to be certain that the plant was still able to function safely. According to a letter written to Senator Boxer by the NRC chairman, Nils J. Diaz, as quoted on the Nuclear.com Web Site,

> Within an hour [of the earthquake], dozens of workers . . . began comprehensive examinations of the plant's foundations and of the station's structures, systems and components to determine if they were damaged. The NRC inspected the plant searching for broken, shifted, or leaking pipes and their support braces; displaced equipment; cracks in cement walls and the plant's foundations, and other signs of damage. No damage was observed by either the [plant's] examinations or the NRC's inspection. Diablo Canyon is constructed and licensed to withstand and operate during an earthquake more powerful than the one of December 22, 2003. In addition, as part of the original plant license, the [owner utility] was required to implement a program to reevaluate the seismic design bases used for the Diablo Canyon Power Plant. This latest earthquake will be evaluated as part of that program.

an earthquake. The NRC also required the plant to install seismic sensors that would automatically shut down the reactor if a certain degree of ground movement was detected.

OTHER ENVIRONMENTAL FACTORS

The NRC also requires that a utility that wants to construct a new nuclear plant should collect meteorological data for at least one year on climate, wind speed, wind direction, and precipitation. This information is important both for plant safety and operation, and in forming emergency plans for the plant. For example, in the event of an inadvertent discharge of radioactivity, it would be very important to know how quickly a discharge would travel to nearby population areas. Planners also need to be fully aware of natural conditions such as unusual amounts of icing in cold weather or the likelihood of tornadoes, flooding, or hurricanes. The plant can then be constructed with extra-thick walls or special systems to deal with high water or ice accumulation.

Ensuring a constant source of water for cooling the plant's reactors is also vital when choosing a site. Many nuclear plants are built on the ocean so they can use ocean water for cooling. Other plants are located on large lakes or rivers. The NRC requires the plants to have enough available water for emergencies as well as for normal operation, and the plant must also be prepared for times of drought or low water levels. For example, when the Duane Arnold Energy Center nuclear plant was constructed in Iowa in the early 1970s, the utility built the plant beside a river and constructed a reservoir a few miles upstream to make sure that the plant would always have enough water for cooling, even during times of drought.

ENVIRONMENTAL IMPACT

A utility that wants to construct a nuclear plant must also study the environmental impact that the plant will have on surrounding areas. This requirement grew from a controversy in the 1960s when environmentalists became concerned about the large amounts of heated water discharged by plants into lakes, rivers, and oceans. Heat can endanger aquatic life that is sensitive to temperature variations. For example, when fish were subjected to a range of water temperatures in laboratory settings, it was discovered that high temperatures lowered the survival rates of both the fish and their eggs.

The problem originated because large amounts of water from the environment were used to condense the steam used to drive the turbines and generate electricity. This water was usually heated by ten to twenty degrees Fahrenheit. It was then returned to the body of water it came from. This process created water that looked, tasted, and smelled unpleasant, as well as being too warm.

This discharge of heated water is called thermal pollution, and the controversy resulted in the enactment of the National Environmental Policy Act in 1969, requiring all utilities to provide an environmental impact statement before they could receive a construction permit for a new power plant. The act was first applied to the nuclear industry before the construction of the Calvert Cliffs Nuclear Plant in Maryland in 1971. The plant was originally going to discharge its heated water into Cayuga Lake, but because of the potential thermal pollution, the utility was required to build large cooling towers through which the heated water circulated before it was discharged into the lake. Other nuclear plants have had to construct cooling ponds to cool their water before it is discharged back into the environment.

One of the major concerns over the construction of the Seabrook Station Nuclear Plant was the nearby clam beds, which were a source of income for local fishermen. They feared

To avoid thermal pollution of the environment, water heated by nuclear reactors must first be cooled in giant cooling towers before being returned to a body of water.

that discharge from the plant and possible thermal pollution from its use of ocean water for cooling would harm the clam beds. The plant was constructed only after a yearlong series of hearings and environmental studies to make sure that the clam beds would not be affected.

Other environmental factors are also considered when siting a nuclear plant, especially the plant's potential impact on any delicate species in the area. According to the NRC's guidelines,

> It should be determined whether there are any important ecological systems at the site or in its environs. If so, determination should be made as to whether the ecological systems are especially vulnerable to change or if they contain important species breeding habitats, such as breeding areas [for nesting and spawning], nursery, feeding, resting, and wintering areas, or other seasonally high concentrations of individuals of important species.[12]

NUCLEAR PLANTS AND POPULATION

Apart from environmental and geological concerns, the most important aspect of determining a nuclear plant's location is the nearby population areas. Nuclear power plants are usually located away from areas of dense population, such as cities, to make emergency planning easier and to limit the potential damage to people and property if an accident should occur. The NRC has a complicated guideline for locating plants a safe distance from any population center of twenty-five thousand inhabitants or more. The plant should also not be located closer than five miles to military bases and industrial areas and ten miles to airports, since the activities associated with these facilities, such as the use of missiles or the shock waves created by air traffic, might be potentially hazardous to a nuclear plant.

Plants should be located in areas that make emergency planning the easiest. Emergency planning consists of developing an extensive plan for evacuating people as quickly and easily as possible in the event of an accident. According to the NRC guidelines, site planning should also consider the following criteria:

> An examination and evaluation of the site and its vicinity, including the population distribution and transportation routes, should be conducted to determine whether there are any characteristics that would pose a signifi-

POWER PLANTS AND ANIMAL POPULATIONS

The NRC's siting guidelines for the construction of nuclear power plants pay a great deal of attention to the well-being of animal species in the area and the plant's possible effects on them. Not only does the NRC require the utility company to perform an ecological sensitivity study, but if the information gathered is not sufficient to determine whether or not the plant should be located there, the NRC will order more extensive studies.

The greatest concern is how the power plant will affect the immediate area. Any places used for animal or bird breeding or nurseries must be studied carefully, because some species return to the same places every year and their breeding and populations may be reduced if these areas are disturbed. Feeding areas that are unique or especially rich cannot be degraded, destroyed, or made inaccessible by the power plant, in case such changes severely harm the populations of certain animals or birds.

The NRC also studies any migratory zones that might be blocked or contaminated by the plant's operations. Rivers and estuaries used by migratory animals must be carefully maintained, because while strong-swimming adult animals might avoid areas where the water is disturbed or of low quality, immature animals or larvae might not be able to keep out of these areas and may be harmed. Intake and discharge structures for the plant must not disrupt the usual migratory patterns.

The NRC also requires that native fish cannot be affected by limited food supplies or abnormal temperatures. Canals or other areas where cooling water is discharged may become an unnaturally warm habitat for fish, reducing the survival rate of both fish and their eggs.

cant impediment to taking protective actions to protect the public in the event of an emergency. Special population groups, such as those in hospitals, prisons, or other facilities that could require special needs during an emergency, should be identified.[13]

The utility must also consider issues like maintaining the appearance of natural resource areas and minimizing noise so as not to disturb nearby residents. The plant should not affect the distinctive character of any neighboring communities, since many people fear that the construction of a nuclear plant will detract from the attractiveness of their neighborhoods. The utility must be especially concerned with those areas with low-income or minority populations, who might be negatively affected by having a nuclear plant in their area because their already low property values might decrease even further.

Permits and Planning

All these site considerations must be met before the NRC will issue a construction permit to the utility for its new nuclear plant. But other factors must also be considered before the plant can be built. Besides site suitability, the permit process for building a nuclear plant also involves safety and antitrust issues. Safety requires the filing of a preliminary safety report, safety reviews done by the NRC staff, and a public hearing. The antitrust issue means making sure that a utility will not have a monopoly over all power production activities in the area, which would limit competition. The antitrust issue requires a decision by the attorney general and the Department of Justice, and a public hearing may be held if needed.

Environmental considerations and site suitability studies will often produce as much as ten volumes of material about the proposed site. Federal, state, and local agencies as well as other

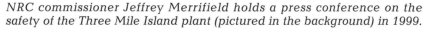

NRC commissioner Jeffrey Merrifield holds a press conference on the safety of the Three Mile Island plant (pictured in the background) in 1999.

interested groups, such as antinuclear or environmental groups, will have a chance to review this material. It is at this stage that public hearings are most likely to attract media attention and protests by local people who are concerned about having a nuclear plant in their neighborhood. Such protests can delay the final decision.

When hearings were held for the construction of Seabrook Station in New Hampshire, local politics and the media complicated the process because the plant's site was near the borders of two other states. The plant's ten-mile emergency planning zone extended across the state line into Massachusetts, but the state did not want to approve the initial emergency planning efforts for Seabrook, because this state felt the plans might not be sufficient. As a result, in 1988 the NRC adopted a realism rule, stating that if state and local agencies refuse to participate in evacuation planning, then the NRC and the Federal Emergency Management Agency can work with the utility to develop these emergency plans. This ruling meant that nuclear plants could still be licensed to operate safely even without state cooperation.

It is important to note that by the time the utility reaches this stage of the approval process, it will have already submitted detailed plans for the plant's design and all its systems, components, and structures, as well as its quality assurance program. The NRC will examine all of this material to see if the proposed plant will be safe and consistent with the NRC's rules and regulations.

If all the findings and reports are positive at this point, the NRC will issue a construction permit so that the plant can actually be built. The length of time it takes from the first permits to operational status for a nuclear power plant averages ten years. This has led to concerns about the delays in the process and the need for more streamlined and consistent approval procedures while still making sure that the plant is safe. Many proposed nuclear plants are never built because of excessive delays in the approval and licensing process.

Once the plant has been given a green light for construction, the actual building will take place. This building process highlights the detailed measures taken to make sure that safety and reliability are paramount in the construction and operation of the plant.

SAFETY ISSUES IN BUILDING NUCLEAR POWER PLANTS

When a nuclear plant has successfully reached the stage of obtaining a construction permit from the Nuclear Regulatory Commission (NRC), the utility can actually begin to build the plant. Although a nuclear power plant's buildings are constructed with the same basic materials and in much the same way that any large modern factory or plant is built, the difference lies in the overall concern with safety in every aspect of the construction process. Safety is also considered first and foremost when developing the plant's operational procedures.

THE LESSONS OF SAFETY

Safety has been a major consideration ever since the first nuclear reactors were built. In 1948, the Atomic Energy Commission (AEC) established the Advisory Committee on Reactor Safeguards (ACRS), whose job it was to oversee and advise the nuclear industry on safety issues and accident prevention. The committee was formed because some people in the scientific community thought that the AEC was not concerned enough with nuclear safety. The ACRS was created to prevent any future loss of life from atomic energy, according to the American Nuclear Society Public Information Committee's Web site on the history of nuclear safety:

> The committee believed that there was no alternative to extreme caution—particularly, given that the images of the aftermath of WW II [and the atomic bombs dropped on Japan] were still on the minds of all people, a single accident in an industrial nuclear reactor could wreck hopes for the peaceful atom. Their service to the AEC was to review every proposal for a reactor. Each pro-

posal required a special evaluation that provided answers to two questions: What is the maximum credible accident? What are the consequences of a maximum credible accident? To answer these questions, the ACRS [realized that] the final guide toward safety had to be experience in actual use.[14]

The result of this reasoning was the ACRS's proposal to the AEC that it build an experimental facility in a deserted location. Here scientists and engineers could make nuclear reactors malfunction in practically any imaginable way without the consequences that would occur if the same malfunction took place in a real nuclear reactor in a populated area. The result of this proposal was the National Reactor Testing Station, established in Arco, Idaho, in 1949.

The National Reactor Testing Station was built on eight hundred square miles of government land, with the purpose of performing advanced research on nuclear systems. Testing on

The domed reactor containment buildings and rings of cooling towers take shape during construction of Arizona's Palo Verde plant.

many different types of nuclear reactors took place here. Because of a shortage of uranium, a breeder reactor (which recycles its fuel for continued use) was constructed and tested. The U.S. Navy tested nuclear propulsions systems for its submarines and ships. In the 1960s, a small reactor was built to test emergency cooling systems in reactors where there might be an accidental loss of coolant. This particular series of tests pointed out that there were serious deficiencies in the nuclear industry's safety standards, and the AEC formed a committee to study the problem.

The National Reactor Testing Station was also the site of a deadly nuclear accident. An experimental type of nuclear reactor, called the SL-1 (Stationary Low Power), was destroyed on January 3, 1961, when three technicians entered the reactor building to do maintenance. A reactor control rod, which was usually manually lifted four inches during maintenance, was accidentally lifted too far. In a millionth of a second, the reactor

Workers at the National Reactor Testing Station in Idaho conduct safety tests. The government facility had a deadly accident in 1961.

A MISSING SCREW

In the daily operation of a nuclear power plant, no detail is too insignificant when it comes to safety. An example of the extreme importance given to the smallest details concerning safety in a nuclear power plant took place in Madrid, Spain, in December 2003. During a refueling outage—the phase when spent fuel is replaced with fresh fuel—a screw less than an inch in diameter was discovered to be missing from a tool used in the refueling process. Because workers did not know where the missing screw fell off, and what systems it might affect, the plant could not go back into operation as planned.

It was feared that the tiny screw might have fallen into the reactor core, even though the manufacturer of the plant systems believed that the screw was too large to fall into the core. Staff at the power plant spent two days searching the reactor vessel that holds the core and dismantled the core itself with a remote-controlled machine in a sealed area. Even searching with remote cameras failed to locate the screw. The nuclear plant is now under investigation and cannot restart until the screw is found.

overheated and melted the nuclear fuel, causing an explosive amount of steam that lifted the reactor vessel off the ground.

Two of the technicians died immediately, one impaled on the ceiling of the reactor building by a control rod. The third technician, who was contaminated with enough radioactive material that the doctor had to wear protective clothing to examine him, died shortly after. The three men's bodies were so radioactive that their hands had to be buried separately with other radioactive waste, and their bodies were buried in lead coffins. The permanent record of one burial, according to the Arlington National Cemetery, warns:

> Victim of nuclear accident. Body is contaminated with long-life radioactive isotopes. Under no circumstances will the body be moved from this location without prior approval of the Atomic Energy Commission in consultation with this headquarters.[15]

The accident was attributed to human error and a design defect. It took eighteen months to decontaminate the reactor building, and the nuclear industry learned many lessons about the safe design of future power plants and the proper training of technicians. The most important lesson learned from the National Reactor Testing Station and its scientists was a better understanding of the precautions that needed to be taken in a commercial nuclear power plant. Lessons learned in Idaho have resulted in some of the requirements that must be met when building and running a nuclear plant.

BUILDING SAFETY INTO A NUCLEAR PLANT

Safety in a nuclear power plant involves a series of four goals: public safety, which means preventing release of radioactive materials in dangerous quantities to the general public; industrial safety, which means eliminating accidents to plant personnel; economic safety, which means minimizing the possibility of a serious accident that would damage the nuclear plant; and operational safety, which means limiting system malfunctions and deviations from normal operations.

All of these goals are considered in the building and eventual operation of a nuclear plant. Referred to as defense in depth, it is a philosophy that calls for multiple layers of protection in a nuclear facility, including the use of multiple barriers to prevent the release of radiation, multiple safety functions, and emergency response measures.

USING CONCRETE IN NUCLEAR CONSTRUCTION

Safety begins with the very materials that are used to construct the plant. The major building material used in a nuclear power plant is concrete. As Richard A. Bradshaw Jr. explains in the book *Construction of Power Generation Facilities*,

> Concrete, in addition to being an excellent structural material, also possesses the required characteristics for . . . an excellent radiation shielding material. Its ease of construction, low initial cost and low maintenance cost are also favorable considerations when choosing a material for radiation shielding.[16]

The use of concrete in the construction of a nuclear plant is especially important in containing radioactive materials. According to the Nuclear Energy Institute in its publication *Guide to Nuclear Energy*,

Pictured is the skeleton of a cooling tower under construction in South Africa. The ultradense concrete used in the tower provides structural strength and radiation protection.

> U.S. nuclear power plants . . . use a series of physical barriers to make sure that radioactive material does not escape. At most plants, the reactor and vessel are enclosed in a large, leak-tight shell of steel plate. All this is contained inside a massive, reinforced-concrete structure—called the containment—with walls that are typically three to four feet thick. The many thick layers of the containment building keep radioactive materials safely inside.[17]

The materials and construction designs of power plants are selected for their ability to withstand potential adverse weather conditions, such as wind or tornadoes. Concrete buildings with a steel framework are best able to endure the high winds of these kinds of weather events. The concrete also allows a plant to withstand earthquakes, as well as incidents such as an airplane flying into the containment building, where the reactor is.

STRUCTURAL SAFETY

One of the biggest fears of many Americans after the terrorist attacks of September 11, 2001, was the possibility of a nuclear plant being struck by an airliner. Many people think that flying an airplane into a power plant would create a nuclear explosion. Not only is this not true, but nuclear power plants have always been constructed to withstand incidents like airplane crashes as part of the licensing process, although it was always assumed that this kind of crash would be accidental and limited to plants located near airports.

If a 767 airliner were to attempt to hit a nuclear power plant and breach the reactor vessel, the plane would face many obstacles. The first is the size of the power plant, which is low to the ground and comparatively small. The average containment building is 140 feet wide and 140 feet tall, compared to the World Trade Center at 208 feet wide and 1,353 feet tall or the Pentagon at 1,489 feet wide and 79 feet tall. Even an experienced pilot would have great difficulty hitting the building at 350 miles per hour, flying low to the ground.

The greatest obstacle is the containment building itself, which is constructed with extremely thick, reinforced concrete walls. Even if a plane or missile breached the walls, the chances of striking the reactor vessel are smaller still since the concrete would deflect the airplane as well as slow it down. In most cases, even striking the reactor vessel would merely cause it to leak water and steam and shut itself down. It is physically impossible for a commercial nuclear reactor to explode like a bomb, because the composition of nuclear fuel used to generate electricity is different from that used in a bomb, and the commercial reactor can only release energy slowly, whereas a bomb must release the energy instantaneously.

According to a study performed by the Electrical Power Research Institute, using sophisticated computer models simulating many different types of crashes into different types of power plants, the fear of terrorism at nuclear plants is unfounded. As Tom Randall of the National Center for Public Policy said in an October 2001 interview with *National Review* magazine, when asked if Americans should worry about living near a nuclear power plant,

> Absolutely not. Recent media scares are completely unfounded. There are tens of thousands of sites . . . which are far more attractive targets for terrorists and would inflict much greater damage and loss of human life. These other targets would also be far easier to attack.

In order to be an efficient shielding material, the concrete mixture used in power plant construction is usually 60 percent denser than regular concrete. But it still can be mixed on the site in the large amounts required for such a big building project. The actual cement used to make the concrete is carefully purchased and stored to make sure that it is free of imperfections and of the high quality necessary. Cement suppliers must pass stringent tests before their material can be used in power plant construction. For example, a sample of the cement is tested in a laboratory for its chemical composition and physical characteristics. The cement is stored on-site in a silo, to prevent anyone from tampering with it and compromising the quality. Later the mixed concrete itself is also tested at the building site. All these precautions ensure that the completed power plant will be built of the highest quality material that will perform according to the plant's design and provide strength and protection from radiation.

USING STEEL IN NUCLEAR CONSTRUCTION

Building a power plant also requires steel, either as reinforcement within the concrete or as the skeleton of the building itself. When contractors construct a nuclear power plant, they cannot simply obtain the steel used in the buildings from any source at the cheapest price. The safety of the public and the longevity of the plant depend on using the finest materials available. According to Denis Mason's article "Steel Fabrication in the Nuclear Power Industry" in the book *Construction of Power Generation Facilities*, "Every action taken [in a steel fabrication facility] that MAY affect the operation or safety of a Nuclear Power Plant must be tested, verified, and certified."[18]

A contractor will not even place an order with a supplier unless it is on the approved vendor list, meaning that the contractor has visited the supplier's factory and audited its quality assurance methods, manufacturing processes, and the certification of its employees. Then the vendor will be issued a certificate of authorization and the contractor will make the purchase.

The raw materials used in steel production must be traceable so that the manufacturer knows exactly where they came from, including when the alloy was created at the foundry. The material is then tested for any flaws and stored in a segregated warehouse area. When it is time to fabricate the raw materials into

Ongoing inspection and testing of the steel and other materials used in constructing nuclear power plants is an important safety measure.

finished steel components, the work can be done only by properly trained and certified employees. Testing takes place throughout the fabrication process and is recorded in documents that will be delivered to the contractor along with the steel. All this verifies that the steel used in construction is the correct type and quality specified by the designing engineers of the power plant. This process is part of what makes the construction of a nuclear power plant so expensive and time-consuming, but it also guarantees that the steel used in the structures is of the best possible quality and ensures that the plant is safe and will maintain its structural integrity throughout its lifetime.

INSPECTING FOR QUALITY

The final assurance of safety in the nuclear plant's actual construction is a rigorous schedule of constant inspections by the NRC. Every stage of the plant's construction is monitored for adherence to the NRC's guidelines before the next stage can proceed. In the past, the NRC sometimes halted progress on a power plant until a problem could be corrected.

The NRC will continue to inspect the plant throughout construction, installation of equipment, and start-up, and throughout the life of the plant. These inspections ensure that all nuclear plants are constructed and maintained properly and allow the NRC to monitor any design or operation problems and address any issues at other plants sharing similar systems.

SAFETY AND NUCLEAR PLANT PERSONNEL

Another built-in safety feature of any nuclear power plant is not made of concrete or steel, but rather consists of properly training the personnel who work at the plant. Plant personnel must be

THE CONTROL ROOM

If the heart of the nuclear power plant is the reactor, then the brain is the control room, where the operators constantly monitor the plant's systems. The NRC has set guidelines concerning control room habitability, to make sure that the control room will be safe for human occupants during both normal operations and emergency situations. The control room is protected from radiation, smoke, chemicals, and fire. It also has a separate air supply, heating and cooling systems, and sanitation facilities. The rooms need to be protected so that the operators can remain at their posts to shut down the reactor in case of an emergency.

The personnel inside the control room at any one time can include a shift manager, shift supervisor, senior reactor operator, reactor operator, assistant reactor operator, and shift technical adviser. The personnel in the control room must be there twenty-four hours a day in two or three work shifts, so that the plant is constantly monitored. Control room personnel go through extensive training to perform their jobs. They begin with thorough classroom training, then proceed to hands-on training with a simulator. The simulator is a full-size replica of the real control room with lights and switches that are connected to a computer. The computer will operate the lights and indicators to provide the trainees with experience in normal and unusual operating situations. They learn the proper procedures for running the plant systems and are trained in emergency scenarios before they begin working at an actual plant. Reactor operators must also be licensed by the NRC to certify that they have been properly trained, and they participate in further training throughout their careers as new procedures are introduced.

educated in every aspect of the plant's function and thoroughly understand the process of obtaining electricity from a nuclear reactor. This overall knowledge is a building block for training in emergency response and preparedness. Nuclear plant employees are not only trained in what to do in the event of an unusual situation, but drilled and graded in emergency scenarios several times a year to make sure that they will know exactly what to do. A scenario can be as simple as malfunctioning equipment and as complex as a release of radioactive materials into the environment. These scenarios sometimes involve the participation of state and county personnel and local hospitals.

A nuclear power plant requires a large department dedicated to training the employees both initially and on a continuing basis. This department is staffed by instructors who conduct training in each specific aspect of plant function. After the Three Mile Island accident in 1979, the nuclear industry created the Institute of Nuclear Power Operations (INPO), to set and police the standards of excellence for training in nuclear plants.

In 1985, the nuclear industry created the National Academy for Nuclear Training, which integrates and standardizes the training programs of INPO and U.S. nuclear plants. The training programs at nuclear plants must be accredited, meaning that inspectors from the National Nuclear Accrediting Board have visited the plant and verified that its training programs meet the standards for the industry. The training programs are not just for the operators, but also for chemists, radiation protection technicians, engineering staff, and other employees. This ensures consistent performance from all site personnel. According to the Nuclear Energy Institute's article "Personnel Training,"

> The industry's training programs have been extremely successful. Since 1979, the number of professional training staff has increased elevenfold, and the space dedicated to training activities has increased eightfold. The investments in training have yielded significant improvements in nuclear plant safety and reliability in the past 20 years.[19]

A nuclear power plant's training department and activities ensure continued safe operation and accident prevention at U.S. nuclear plants. A similar organization in Russia's Chernobyl plant might have prevented the catastrophic accident that took place there.

THE CHERNOBYL ACCIDENT

The world's worst nuclear energy plant accident occurred on April 26, 1986, at the Chernobyl nuclear power plant in the Ukraine, in what was then the Soviet Union but is now Russia. Chernobyl was a graphite-moderated reactor, a type of reactor that is not used in U.S. nuclear power plants. Chernobyl's plant also did not have a concrete containment dome like those built on all U.S. plants.

The Chernobyl accident occurred when two explosions only seconds apart blew off the reactor's roof, started fires, and forced radioactive gases into the atmosphere. The accident was due to plant design weaknesses and operator error: The reactor did not have a strong enough containment building, the reactor could not shut down quickly, and the operators could too easily override the safety systems. The overall operating system was difficult to control, and mistakes made by the operators led to a situation in which the emergency systems had been shut down

An instructor observes as a control room trainee handles a simulated emergency. Plant employees participate in plant-wide emergency drills several times each year.

In 2004 a Ukrainian woman sets a photo of her son at a memorial to honor those who died in the 1986 accident at the Chernobyl nuclear power plant.

and a power surge caused explosions. The plant controls had also been left in the hands of an electrical engineer with no previous experience at a nuclear power plant.

It took 186 firemen to control the fire burning in the reactor, where the reactor core was blown outside of the reactor vault. Many of these firemen died from radiation poisoning in the next few weeks. Because the core continued to heat up (and may have at one time reached temperatures as high as four thousand degrees Fahrenheit), Russian air force planes flew over the site and dropped five thousand tons of lead, sand, and clay to bring the temperature down.

A huge cloud of radioactive particles drifted over several European countries, but because of the political situation at the time, the Soviet authorities did not inform anyone of the accident until Swedish scientists identified the cloud and demanded an explanation. The Soviets admitted that there had been a nuclear accident but refused to release any other information. As of December 2000, the NRC reported that thirty-one people died in the Chernobyl accident, most of whom were fighting fires that resulted from the accident. The long-term health effects have not yet been officially determined. One hundred thirty thousand people from the Chernobyl area were resettled.

Chernobyl's accident could not take place in the United States, with its stricter regulations and different types of nuclear plants, but it was a reminder that nuclear power must be used responsibly. As Vice President Al Gore said in a statement at the Chernobyl plant in July 1998, "The lesson of Chernobyl is not an indictment of nuclear power as such. Nuclear power, designed well, regulated properly, cared for meticulously, has a place in the world's energy supply."[20]

BUILT-IN SAFETY SYSTEMS

A nuclear plant does not rely only on the building construction and the plant personnel for safety in operation. The plant equipment has many built-in safety systems that automatically shut down the reactor under certain conditions, all of which add to the complexity of building a nuclear plant. These systems involve piping, electrical work, and ductwork, and their placement must be carefully included in the building designs of the plant. These systems are designed to remove heat and reduce excess pressure if an accident should occur, maintaining the integrity of the reactor vessel and its fuel and keeping it from cracking due to high heat. Plant operators can flood the reactor core with water and keep it filled to cool it, spray down the outside of the reactor with water, or inject water into the reactor at high or low pressure. There are also systems of filters, vents, scrubbers, and air circulators that can collect and retain certain radioactive gases and particles before they are released to the environment. These systems can all be controlled by reactor operators from the safety of the plant's control room.

Other systems automatically shut down the reactor in the event of fire in the plant. The system will also shut down the reactor if the turbines, which convert the steam from the reactor into electricity, should fail, in which case there would be nowhere for the reactor power to go. Any automatic shutdown due to an unsafe condition is called a "scram," and it is cause for detailed inspections and assessments of all systems before the plant can be started up again.

A plant is required to formally announce any events that occur at the plant, and these are often reported in the media even when they are nonevents, because anything to do with nuclear power attracts public attention. This was the case at the Seabrook Station nuclear plant in November 2003. Workers fixed a small hydrogen leak in the turbine generator, which is located in a separate building from the nuclear reactor. A small brass plug was found to be loose and a small amount of nonradioactive hydrogen was released into the atmosphere. The plant declared an Unusual Event, which is the lowest of four emergency classifications at the plant. The event was declared at 9:08 A.M. and was over immediately, also at 9:08 A.M. An account of this nonevent appeared in local newspapers and television.

The safety requirements in operating a nuclear power plant were even further refined after Three Mile Island, an event that shook the U.S. public's faith in the safety of nuclear power.

THREE MILE ISLAND

Three Mile Island was one of the United States' most publicized nuclear accidents. When most people think about nuclear power plants and potential safety issues, they think about Three Mile Island, which is a two-unit plant located in the middle of the Susquehanna River in Pennsylvania. On March 28, 1979, the reactor experienced a loss of cooling water. The reactor overheated, and because the emergency core cooling system had been shut off at some point, water no longer covered the nuclear fuel and some of the fuel rods melted and ruptured. This resulted in the release of radioactive gases into the atmosphere and severe damage to the reactor. Pregnant women and preschool children within a one-mile radius of the plant were evacuated. Eventually cooling was restored and conditions returned to normal. Recently, accident analysts have come to believe that the release of radiation was actually at a much smaller level than had first been assumed, too small a level to result in any discernible health effects.

The accident at Three Mile Island was important because it pointed out some of the weaknesses in the power plant's design and operation. Investigators determined that reactor operators required more training, sparking the creation of the Institute of Nuclear Power Operations (INPO) to establish guidelines for excellence for power plant operation. Because it led to the creation of INPO and an in-depth review of power plant safety, Three Mile Island was responsible for increasing the safety of nuclear power plants, even though public fears about nuclear power increased.

The nuclear industry also realized that better emergency communication was needed, as well as technical improvements to better monitor reactor conditions. Plant owners and managers have since learned to communicate with each other as well as with the NRC about safety issues that may pertain to more than one nuclear facility. In 2001, when two power plants

A civil defense worker monitors radiation with a Geiger counter as school-children are evacuated after the Three Mile Island nuclear accident in 1979.

THE CHINA SYNDROME

Of all the potential dangers of nuclear power, the China Syndrome has been one of the most well publicized. The China Syndrome is the hypothesis that a nuclear reactor could go out of control and become so hot that it would melt down through Earth's crust to Earth's core itself. Scientists on the Advisory Committee on Reactor Safeguards had already seriously considered this possibility as early as the mid-1960s. This committee looked at several scenarios that might result in a reactor catastrophe. It also asked the nuclear industry to come up with a better emergency system to prevent the possibility of a drastic meltdown. The safeguards that already exist in a nuclear plant, however, would prevent this scenario from ever taking place.

The China Syndrome received even more notoriety in 1979 when a movie of the same name was made. It was loosely based on several incidents at the Rancho Seco power plant in California, and in the movie the power plant did shut down exactly as it was designed to do. The movie was still playing at the time of the Three Mile Island accident, gaining additional notoriety, but it is interesting to note that although the reactor at that plant suffered a partial meltdown, nothing even resembling the China Syndrome took place.

found a certain type of corrosion in their reactor vessel head, the NRC issued a bulletin to all nuclear plants with a specific list of inspections to be made on their equipment to look for a similar problem. When the Davis-Besse Nuclear Power Station in Ohio performed the inspection during its next refueling outage, it found a tremendous amount of corrosion that could have compromised reactor safety. It was because of the NRC's increased communication with plants that the problem was addressed before it became worse.

PLANNING FOR EMERGENCIES

Another important aspect of public safety in the construction and operation of a nuclear plant is the emergency planning that must be in place before the plant can even operate. The NRC has a specific list of components that must be addressed in a plant's emergency plan, including a strategy to cope with radiation emergencies. The plant must have notification procedures, such as a system of sirens and a means for alerting local emergency officials. There must be emergency facilities and equipment, and personnel must be trained in emergency procedures. This involves frequent drills to make sure that plant workers are always prepared for an emergency.

Each plant must also have a procedure in place for an emergency evacuation of the surrounding area if necessary. Each plant has an Emergency Planning Zone (EPZ), which is determined for each plant depending on its location, the characteristics of the

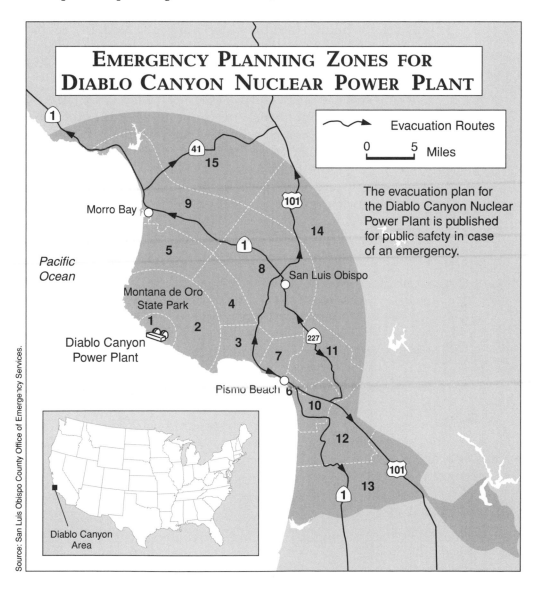

EMERGENCY PLANNING ZONES FOR DIABLO CANYON NUCLEAR POWER PLANT

Evacuation Routes

0 — 5 Miles

The evacuation plan for the Diablo Canyon Nuclear Power Plant is published for public safety in case of an emergency.

Morro Bay

Pacific Ocean

San Luis Obispo

Montana de Oro State Park

Diablo Canyon Power Plant

Pismo Beach

Diablo Canyon Area

Source: San Luis Obispo County Office of Emergency Services.

land, and access routes. For most plants, the EPZ for its plume (meaning how far any airborne emission from the plant could drift) is approximately ten miles in radius. The EPZ for ingestion (contamination of any food or animal products that could be ingested by the public) is approximately fifty miles in radius. With these zones in mind, the plant will cooperate with local officials to create an evacuation program for moving and temporarily relocating inhabitants of these areas. This usually involves a comprehensive plan for transporting people, especially schoolchildren and the elderly and disabled, to specific relocation areas in other towns out of the EPZ. In many communities, this information is published in the local phone book and on the plant's Web site for easy access by the public.

All these aspects of safety—structural safeguards, trained personnel, cooperation from the community, and automated safety systems—are combined in the building and operating of a nuclear plant to make sure that it not only produces electricity but protects the public as well. Although some of these safety lessons were learned the hard way, through deadly accidents, the nuclear industry is safer now than ever before. The ability to provide safe nuclear power may be a powerful influence as America enters the twenty-first century and the issue of providing enough power becomes more critical.

The Future of Nuclear Power

After the incidents at Three Mile Island and Chernobyl, nuclear power plants were no longer built with such frequency, due to public worries about the safety of nuclear power and the increasing costs of constructing the plants. Industry regulation had become so complicated that utilities had to go through years of hearings, research, and paperwork to construct these plants. In the decade of the 1990s, only five new nuclear power plants began commercial operations in the United States, and new plants typically take ten years from planning to completion. In fact, new plants are not being built in the United States until the regulation process becomes more streamlined.

A Sea of Regulations

The reasons why new nuclear plants are not currently being built include the costs and regulations involved in siting, licensing, and operating new plants and the high cost of constructing existing nuclear reactor designs. Many regulations were introduced after the Three Mile Island incident, as the Nuclear Regulatory Commission (NRC) made sure that the lessons learned from that plant were applied to licensing new plants. Unfortunately, it now takes so long for a new plant to get a construction permit and an operating license, and the costs for all the inspections, testing, and required features have increased so much, that nuclear plant construction cannot keep up with the country's electricity needs.

In addition to the NRC's regulations, there are also at least seventeen federal laws that apply to nuclear plants, including the Atomic Energy Act of 1954, the Endangered Species Act of 1973, the Toxic Substances Control Act of 1976, the Clean Air Act of 1977, and the Power Plant and Industrial Fuel Use Act of 1978.

Many utilities and contractors now think that with so many laws and regulations to follow, nuclear energy is not a realistic option for a power plant. According to William G. Counsil in *Construction of Power Generation Facilities*,

> [There is a] heavy burden of statutes, permits and regulations that the utility industry must bear. In the case of the NRC, this has led to the current regulatory morass which has effectively removed the "nuclear option" as a viable means for planning our future electrical generation requirements.[21]

A colleague, Russell J. Christensen, adds in the same book:

> The secret to improving performance in construction of power generation facilities is . . . complex because we

In 1989 citizens of Sacramento voted to decommission California's Rancho Seco Nuclear Power Plant and convert it to a solar power plant.

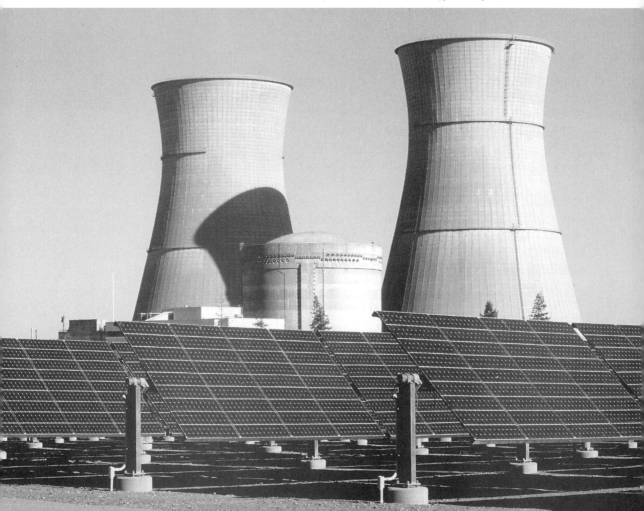

THE ABYSS

A creative use was found for an abandoned nuclear power plant construction site at the Cherokee Nuclear Power Station in Gaffney, South Carolina. Cherokee was never finished and never even reached the low-power testing stage, so it was never contaminated with any radioactive material.

In 1989, Cherokee was used in the filming of the movie *The Abyss*, which takes place deep in the ocean. For the underwater sequences of the movie, Cherokee's nuclear reactor containment building and the turbine pit were converted into underwater filming tanks. One tank was capable of holding over 7 million gallons of water, and the other held 2.5 million gallons, making these tanks the largest heated freshwater tanks in existence.

have so entangled ourselves in a web of restrictions, constraints, standards, guidelines and controls that . . . it will be hard to shake ourselves loose.[22]

A QUESTION OF MONEY

Several nuclear power plants were either built but never used, or left unfinished, because of changing regulatory requirements, inflated construction expenses, or public opposition. Most of these issues came down to the cost of building a plant. The most well-known example is the Shoreham Nuclear Power Station in New York State. Shoreham was awarded a construction license in 1973, and from the beginning it experienced almost every possible problem in the building process. The original price tag of $65 million eventually rose to $5.5 billion. Design flaws and construction errors resulted in parts of the plant being rebuilt several times, and the containment system had to be strengthened when the NRC determined that it had potentially serious design problems. Federal regulations were changing so quickly that the construction of the plant could not keep up with them. When the plant prepared the required comprehensive emergency evacuation plan, state and local authorities raised doubts that the area could be safely evacuated.

The plant was technically complete in 1984 and went through low-power testing, in which nuclear fuel is loaded into the reactor and the reactor is run at a low level to ensure that

After the original cost of New York's Shoreham Nuclear Power Station rose from $65 million to $5.5 billion, the plant became too expensive to operate.

all the systems are working. This meant that the plant could not be abandoned without going through the lengthy, costly process of decommissioning. The utility finally decided, after years of controversy and extreme costs, that it would stop trying to operate the plant. For three years, it was forced to keep the plant in a state of suspended animation, at a cost of $400,000 a day, until the NRC authorized the decommissioning of the plant. Shoreham never produced any electricity, and it is still in the process of being decommissioned, which will cost over $186 million even though the plant only had a relatively small amount of radioactive contamination from its low-power testing. Many people believe that if the Shoreham plant was producing electricity, it could alleviate some of the power shortages that have affected New York City, including the Northeast blackout of 2003.

SPENT NUCLEAR FUEL

Another issue affecting the increased use of nuclear power in the United States is sparking another controversy of its own. This issue is the storage and disposal of nuclear waste, and it is now the greatest problem limiting the growth of the nuclear power industry.

Approximately every eighteen to twenty-four months, a nuclear power plant must be refueled. Uranium fuel becomes depleted through the fission process and can no longer sustain a nuclear reaction. The used fuel bundles must be removed from

Workers place spent fuel rods into a storage pool inside the power plant. Disposal of spent fuel is a major problem with nuclear power.

the reactor and new fresh fuel placed in it. The spent fuel is placed in a spent fuel pool within the power plant itself, but in most U.S. nuclear plants, this storage space is limited. Some plants have constructed storage silos on-site, but the number of silos that can be built at a plant site is also limited. The question of what to do with spent nuclear fuel is becoming urgent.

Spent fuel is not the only nuclear waste that must be disposed of. There are also millions of gallons of high-level (highly radioactive) waste left over from processing plutonium, and millions of cubic feet of low-level contaminated tools, metal scraps, clothing, oils, and solvents from nuclear facilities. There are even the sealed hulls from nuclear propulsion submarines, emptied of fuel but still contaminated with radioactivity.

Initially, the question of where to put the spent fuel was the government's responsibility, according to the Nuclear Energy Institute's *Guide to Nuclear Energy*:

> From the beginning of commercial nuclear energy, it has been national policy that the federal government has responsibility for retaining control and disposing of used fuel. But more than 18 years after Congress created this requirement, the U.S. Department of Energy has refused to meet its contractual obligation to take possession of used fuel. . . . The Energy Department claims that it cannot take the used fuel because the federal government has no place to store it. Hence, a vigorous effort to ensure action on the part of the federal government is the key to maximizing the benefits that society derives from commercial nuclear power plants in the 21st century. This will guarantee that plants will not have to shut down prematurely because a utility has run out of space to store used fuel.[23]

YUCCA MOUNTAIN, NEVADA

The government's response to the problem of storing nuclear waste has been to select Yucca Mountain in Nevada, ninety miles northwest of Las Vegas, as the site for a permanent nuclear waste storage facility. Yucca Mountain is being planned as a repository for nuclear waste from all commercial nuclear power plants in the United States, as well as from other sources. Seventy-seven thousand tons of nuclear waste from both power

A worker walks along a tunnel deep beneath Nevada's Yucca Mountain, which the government has designated as a permanent nuclear waste storage facility.

plants and nuclear weapons would be buried at Yucca Mountain. Placed in specially designed containers, the waste would be buried in a series of tunnels 990 feet below the top of the mountain, but 900 feet above the water table. Almost two thousand workers would be employed.

Many scientists oppose the plant, citing the possibility of earthquakes in the region and possible damage to the water table. The state of Nevada has been fighting the federal government's decision, as described by Michael E. Long in *National Geographic*:

> Adamantly, the state of Nevada finds "significant and unacceptable risks" just about everywhere it looks in Yucca Mountain, from geology to groundwater to nickel alloy containers (for spent fuel) that DOE [Department of Energy] says will last at least 10,000 years. More like 500, says Nevada, and many environmentalists agree. Senator John Ensign [said,] "The Department of Energy has been hell-bent on building Yucca Mountain no matter what the science, what the ethics, what the cost."[24]

The cost for Yucca Mountain is considerable. The Department of Energy has already invested $4 billion testing and tunneling in Yucca Mountain. In November 2003, the U.S. House and Senate approved a $27.3 billion energy and water development appropriations bill that boosts spending for Yucca Mountain and for nuclear research and development in 2004. According to John Kane, senior vice president of governmental affairs for the Nuclear Energy Institute, "This will go a long way toward helping the Department of Energy meet its goal of submitting a license application for the planned [Yucca Mountain] repository to the NRC in December 2004."[25]

TRANSPORTING NUCLEAR WASTE

The other controversy surrounding the use of Yucca Mountain for spent fuel storage involves the transportation of the fuel from the power plants to the storage site. Most commercial nuclear plants are located in the eastern half of the United States, which means that used fuel must travel by truck or railroad to Nevada.

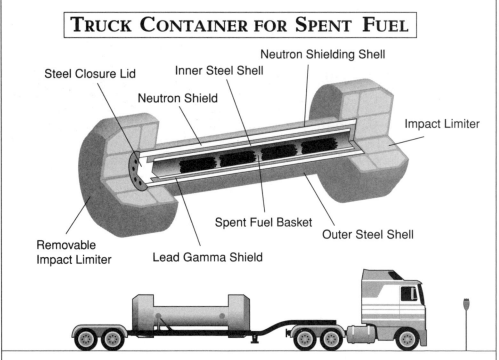

TRUCK CONTAINER FOR SPENT FUEL

Steel Closure Lid
Inner Steel Shell
Neutron Shielding Shell
Neutron Shield
Impact Limiter
Spent Fuel Basket
Outer Steel Shell
Removable Impact Limiter
Lead Gamma Shield

Source: www.nrc.gov/waste/spent-fuel-transp.html.

Many people are concerned about the safety issues involved in transporting radioactive waste for such long distances. This issue also affects the construction of new plants because residents are concerned about waste being transported in their areas. The packaging and transportation of nuclear waste, however, are highly regulated. The truck drivers and other transportation specialists are specially certified and licensed and must plan their route according to Federal Highway Administration regulations, which include avoiding large cities.

The containers used for shipping nuclear waste are constructed from steel with a lead lining for radiation shielding. The NRC certifies all shipping container designs, and they must meet rigorous engineering and safety criteria. The containers are subjected to extensive tests to make sure that they will stand up to traffic accidents and other on-road situations. The containers are tested in potentially damaging situations such as undergoing a free fall onto a hard surface, a fall onto a steel rod, being exposed to fire, and being submersed in water. The containers are subjected to these tests in sequence, meaning that all these tests are performed one after the other on the same container, which is unlikely to ever happen in a real accident.

According to the Nuclear Energy Institute's Web site on safe nuclear fuel transportation, independent laboratories have done even more tests to simulate actual traffic situations:

> In the 1970s and 1980s, engineers and scientists at Sandia National Laboratories in New Mexico subjected used nuclear fuel containers to actual accidents to see what would happen in real-world conditions. Among other accidents, (1) a flatbed tractor-trailer carrying a container was run into a 700-ton concrete wall banked with 1,700 tons of dirt at 80 miles per hour, (2) a container on a tractor-trailer was broadsided by a rocket-assisted 120-ton train locomotive traveling 80 miles per hour, and (3) a container was dropped 2,000 feet onto soil as hard as concrete, traveling 235 miles an hour at impact. In all these cases, the containers survived intact. Post-crash assessments demonstrated that the containers would not have released their contents.[26]

Since 1965, there have been more than two thousand shipments of spent nuclear fuel in the United States without a single

BLACKOUTS AND BROWNOUTS

In the last several years, two incidents have caused the public and the government to think harder about using nuclear energy for electrical generation. These incidents were the California brownouts of 2001 and the Northeast blackout of August 2003.

The California brownouts were a result of a combination of factors, including the inability of the electrical system to supply enough power for the state. The Northeast blackout was due to a failure in the aging energy distribution system. The failure started in Ohio and spread until it encompassed New York, Vermont, Massachusetts, Connecticut, New Jersey, Pennsylvania, Michigan, and parts of Canada.

These incidents have made many people look at nuclear power with renewed interest. President Bush and other politicians think that the United States should consider nuclear energy as a clean source of power, and one without any dependence on foreign sources for its production. The nuclear industry would like to see less complicated processes for construction and licensing. No new nuclear power plant has been put into production since 1996, and dozens of nuclear plant construction plans have been canceled. However, the way to prevent future power shortages and outages may be to further utilize nuclear power in the production of electricity in the United States.

injury or environmental accident. Although many people worry that shipments of used nuclear fuel traveling through their neighborhoods will subject them to radiation, according to the Nuclear Energy Institute the risk of this is extremely low:

> You would receive as much radiation from eating bananas as would a pedestrian watching a year's worth of used nuclear fuel shipments pass by. Even bananas are a source of radiation due to traces of natural-occurring radioactive potassium. Using the maximum estimates of the number of shipments of used nuclear fuel and the levels of radiation that might be present, a person standing by a roadside while an entire year of shipments of spent nuclear fuel passed by his or her location would receive the same amount of radiation as the average American from eating bananas (about 1–2 bananas per week)—1 millirem.[27]

Whether nuclear power plants can continue to meet the ever-increasing energy needs of the United States in the future will depend on finding a way to store used nuclear fuel safely.

POWER PLANT "UNBUILDING"

Most nuclear power plants are not meant to operate indefinitely. There comes a time when every plant must be taken out of service, or decommissioned. Planning for this eventuality is an expensive process that may also affect the construction of new plants.

Nuclear power plants are unique in that their owners must plan for the "unbuilding," or decommissioning, of the plant before it is even constructed. Nuclear plants in the United States are licensed to operate for forty years. When the utility decides to close a nuclear plant permanently, the plant must be decommissioned according to NRC regulations. Decommissioning involves cleaning up any plant systems and structures that are contaminated with radioactivity and removing any nuclear fuel.

When a utility decides to decommission a plant, it must submit a written certificate to the NRC for permanent cessation of operation. When the nuclear fuel is permanently removed from the reactor vessel, the utility submits another certificate, which means that it has permanently lost the authority to operate the reactor or load fuel into it. The utility also holds a public meeting to inform the community of decommissioning and related activities.

There are three different types of decommissioning. They are known by their NRC designations of DECON, SAFESTOR, and ENTOMB. The first is DECON, which is immediate dismantling of the plant. Any contaminated structures or equipment are removed or decontaminated as soon as the plant closes and the NRC operating license can be terminated and the property released for other uses. Another term for this type of decommissioning is *rubblization*: All equipment is removed from the buildings and the surfaces are decontaminated; then all aboveground structures are demolished into rubble and buried in the structure's foundation. The site's surface is then covered, regraded, and landscaped for future nonnuclear uses.

SAFESTOR is often considered a delayed form of DECON: The nuclear facility is maintained until the radioactivity has decayed (anywhere between sixty and three hundred years), and

In 1990 New York officials discuss how to decommission the Shoreham plant in the most cost-effective manner.

then the plant is dismantled. The ENTOMB option involves entombing any radioactive contaminants in concrete or other structurally sound material, and maintaining and monitoring the plant until radioactivity decays to a safe level. Utility owners may also use a combination of decommissioning methods on different areas of the plant site.

The contaminated radioactive equipment that is removed from the site of a decommissioned plant will be treated like other forms of nuclear waste and safely stored in a licensed radioactive waste disposal facility. When the Yankee Rowe Nuclear Power Plant in Monroe, Massachusetts, was dismantled in 1996, the reactor vessel was loaded onto a truck and then a railroad car to be transported to South Carolina for storage in a low-level radioactive waste disposal facility. According to the Yankee Rowe Web site,

> The reactor vessel, which held the fuel that generated more than 33 billion kilowatt-hours of electricity over 31 years, had been removed from the plant's containment building last November [1996]. The 165-ton vessel was placed inside a 3-inch thick, 100 ton steel container certified by the NRC for transport. It was then injected with about 80 tons of concrete and the lid was welded onto the container.
>
> [The container was then loaded onto a truck.] Flanked by Yankee personnel, it made its way slowly—a little more than one mile per hour—into the town of Monroe where

State police escort the Yankee Rowe station's reactor vessel as it is transported to a storage site in South Carolina.

curious residents were out on the sidewalks to watch it pass by. . . . Arriving at the rail spur ahead of schedule . . . over the next two days employees removed the transporter tie downs and hydraulically transferred and secured the package to the rail car. The rail car . . . was chosen because it was designed to transport large, heavy loads and has the ability to shift the load from side to side to clear obstacles. On Tuesday, April 29, 1997, the train left the rail spur and entered the [five-mile-long] Hoosac Tunnel amid waves and cheers from all who had worked so hard to reach this milestone.[28]

The train took eight days and nights to reach South Carolina from Massachusetts. Every rail company that owned tracks along the route provided a security escort for the train, which ran only during daylight hours and was held over in secure rail yards each night. The only obstacles on the entire trip were a few protesters, a handful of cows that had to be herded away from the tracks, and the news media filming from helicopters.

The cost of decommissioning a nuclear plant can be over $100 million, but the utility collects and banks these funds over the lifetime of the plant so as to be prepared for the decommissioning process. The decommissioning must be completed within sixty years, although the entire ENTOMB process may require much more time for the radioacitivty to decay. In the United States, there are currently nineteen nuclear power plants that have shut down and are in various stages of decommissioning. Decommissioning also contributes to the amount of nuclear waste that must be disposed of as well as to the overall expense of a new plant. These issues keep new plants from being built.

Tomorrow's Nuclear Energy

The question of whether or not to build new nuclear power plants in the United States is also dependent on politics and public opinion. Politicians know that nuclear energy is an emotional subject for the public because many people fear it, so the politicians are reluctant to jeopardize their own political futures by supporting the construction of new plants. The outcome of the nuclear power question, however, could have serious consequences for U.S. energy needs.

SEABROOK'S SECOND DOME

In 1976, when construction began on the Seabrook Station nuclear power plant, one of the last nuclear plants built in America, the owner utility, Public Service of New Hampshire, originally planned to build a power plant site with two reactors. Because of the public opposition to the plant and the utility's financial problems, construction on the second reactor stopped in 1984. Although Seabrook's first reactor went online in 1990 and continues to operate, the second abandoned 17.5-foot-high dome has been called an eyesore by the community.

In June 2003, Seabrook's new owner, Florida Power and Light, made the decision to dismantle the second dome and sell it for scrap metal. The equipment inside the dome, including the reactor vessel, which was never loaded with nuclear fuel, will be used for another power plant or sold. A scrap company will remove the panels that make up the steel dome, cut them into pieces, and truck them away.

According to the U.S. Department of Energy,

Electricity demand in the United States is expected to grow sharply in the 21st century requiring new generation capacity. Forecasts indicate that the United States will need about 393,000 megawatts of new generating capacity by [the year] 2020. Nuclear power plants generate twenty percent of the electric energy produced in the United States. Despite the excellent recent performance of nuclear power plants and the decisions by plant owners to seek license renewal and power uprates for existing power plants, no nuclear plants have been ordered in the United States for more than 25 years.[29]

Public fears about nuclear power and the fears of terrorism since September 11, 2001, have also contributed to the stalled construction of nuclear plants. Public concern over the impact of terrorist activities on nuclear power plants and nuclear waste has made it more difficult for utilities to get the approval they need for new plants. Yet the continuing unrest in the Middle East, which impacts U.S. supplies of foreign oil, and the recent energy shortages, such as the brownouts that hit California in 2001 and the Northeast blackout of August 2003, serve as reminders that the United States needs to further develop its sources of electricity.

ADVOCATING NUCLEAR POWER

The U.S. Department of Energy has developed a plan called Nuclear Power 2010 to enhance the electrical generation capacity of the country by building new nuclear power plants, developing advanced nuclear technologies, and creating new regulatory processes. This plan would lead to the deployment of new nuclear plants by the year 2010. The government and the nuclear industry will share the cost of this plan.

The energy appropriations bill passed by Congress in November 2003 also earmarks money to expand the use of nuclear energy, providing $393 million for programs such as the Advanced Fuel Cycle Initiative, the Nuclear Energy Technologies program, the Nuclear Energy Research Initiative, and the Nu-

Most of Manhattan lies in darkness during the August 2003 blackout. The blackout brought into sharp focus the need to explore alternative energy sources such as nuclear power.

clear Plant Optimization program. These programs will fund new forms of nuclear energy that will produce less waste or even reuse their spent fuel.

Older nuclear power plants are also applying for relicensing, which extends their license to operate for a longer period of time than was originally planned for at the time of construction. Most plants are originally licensed for forty years, and a license extension will usually increase this by another twenty years.

Nuclear energy, like all other forms of power generation, has its negative aspects, but many people believe that the ability of the United States to continue to enjoy unlimited electricity for use in homes and businesses will depend heavily on constructing more nuclear power plants. As Idaho senator Larry Craig said in a press release in October 2002:

> As the Senate debates military action in the Middle East, and as our nation has become far too dependent on foreign sources of energy, it is clear that increased domestic energy production is critical to our economic and national security. While all energy sources are important, it is obvious to me that nuclear power plays an especially vital role. Nuclear power offers great benefits, but also poses tremendous challenges. I believe the American government has a clear role to help remove the barriers to an expanded role for nuclear power.[30]

NOTES

Introduction

1. Edison Electric Institute, *Nuclear Power: Answers to Your Questions*. Washington, DC: Edison Electric Institute, 1987, p. 7.

2. World Energy Council/Conseil Mondial de L'Energie, *Energy for Tomorrow's World—Acting Now!*, 2000. www.nei.org/doc.asp?catnum=2&catid=117.

Chapter 1: The Birth of Nuclear Power

3. Quoted in Robert Martin, "The History of Nuclear Power Plant Safety: The Forties," American Nuclear Society Public Information Committee, http://users/owt.com/smsrpm/nksafe/forties.html.

4. Dwight D. Eisenhower, "Atoms for Peace," UN General Assembly, 1953. www.iaea.or.at/worldatom/About/ atoms.html.

5. Robert Martin, "The History of Nuclear Power Plant Safety: The Fifties," American Nuclear Society Public Information Committee, http://users/owt.com/smsrpm/nksafe/fifties.html.

6. Stephen E. Atkins, *Historical Encyclopedia of Atomic Energy*. Westport, CT: Greenwood Press, 2000, pp. 401–402.

Chapter 2: Inside a Nuclear Power Plant

7. Atkins, *Historical Encyclopedia of Atomic Energy*, p 210.

8. Atkins, *Historical Encyclopedia of Atomic Energy*, p. 43.

9. Edison Electric Institute, *Nuclear Power: Answers to Your Questions*, p. 30.

Chapter 3: Finding a Site for a Nuclear Power Plant

10. Quoted in David Dinsmore Comey, "The Fire at Brown's Ferry Nuclear Power Station," Canadian Coalition for Nuclear Responsibility, 1976. www.ccnr.org/browns-ferry.html.

11. U.S. Nuclear Regulatory Commission, "Who We Are," 2003. www.nrc.gov/who-we-are.html.

12. U.S. Nuclear Regulatory Commission, *Regulatory Guide 4.7: General Site Suitability Criteria for Nuclear Power Stations*, 1998 revision, p. 16.

13. U.S. Nuclear Regulatory Commission, *Regulatory Guide 4.7*, p. 14.

Chapter 4: Safety Issues in Building Nuclear Power Plants

14. Robert Martin, "The History of Nuclear Power Plant Safety," American Nuclear Society Public Information Committee. http://users/owt.com/smsrpm/nksafe/about.html.

15. Wolf Sterling, "The SL-1 Reactor," Radiationworks. www.radiationworks.com/sl1reactor.htm.

16. Quoted in Jack H. Willenbrock, ed., *Construction of Power Generation Facilities: Experience with the Implementation of Construction Practices, Codes, Standards and Regulations.* New York: American Society of Civil Engineers, 1982, p. 185.

17. Nuclear Energy Institute, *Guide to Nuclear Energy.* Washington, DC: Nuclear Energy Institute, 2001, p. 6.

18. Quoted in Willenbrock, *Construction of Power Generation Facilities*, p. 396.

19. Nuclear Energy Institute, "Personnel Training." www.nei.org/doc.asp?catnum=3&catid=47&docid=&format.

20. Albert Gore, "The Lesson of Chernobyl," speech, July 1998. www.nei.org/doc.asp?docid=651.

Chapter 5: The Future of Nuclear Power

21. Quoted in Willenbrock, *Construction of Power Generation Facilities*, p. 23.

22. Quoted in Willenbrock, *Construction of Power Generation Facilities*, p. 40.

23. Nuclear Energy Institute, *Guide to Nuclear Energy*, p. 13.

24. Michael E. Long, "America's Nuclear Waste," *National Geographic*, July 2002, pp. 31–32.

25. Quoted in Nuclear Energy Institute, "Congress Approves Energy Appropriations Bill; Yucca Mountain and Nuclear R & D Benefit," 2003. www.nei.org/doc.asp?catnum=2&catid=287&docid=&format.

26. Nuclear Energy Institute, "Nuclear Fuel Transportation Containers Tested for Safety," 2004. www.nei.org/index.asp?catnum=2&catid=81.

27. Nuclear Energy Institute, "Used Nuclear Fuel Shipments: Public Safe from Radiation," www.nei.org/doc.asp?catnum=2&catid=243.

28. Yankee Rowe Nuclear Power Station, "Decommissioning: Reactor Vessel Shipment," 1997. www.yankee.com/decommissioning_removal.html.

29. U.S. Department of Energy, Office of Nuclear Energy, Science and Technology, "Nuclear Power Systems: Nuclear Power 2010." http://www.ne.doe.gov/NucPwr2010/ NucPwr 2010.html.

30. Larry Craig, "Craig Convenes Nuclear Meeting with Vice President and Energy Secretary," press release, October 2002. http://craig.senate.gov/releases/pr100802a.htm.

GLOSSARY

atom: The smallest component of an element that retains the characteristics of that element.

atomic bomb: A bomb whose power comes from a fission chain reaction.

blackout: An electrical power failure during which the only sources of illumination are candles or emergency power.

breeder reactor: A nuclear reactor in which the amount of fuel produced is greater than the amount consumed.

brownout: A reduction in power available for illumination, causing lights to dim.

circulating water: Water originating from a river, lake, or ocean that circulates through a condenser to draw heat from steam, then travels to a cooling tower where it gives up its heat and is then returned to the condenser.

condenser: A component downstream of a turbine that uses tubes cooled by circulating water to change exhaust steam to liquid for reuse by the system.

construction permit: A permit issued by the Nuclear Regulatory Commission allowing construction to begin on a nuclear power plant.

containment building: The structure enclosing the reactor pressure vessel and nuclear fuel, designed to contain any liquid or vapor that might accidentally escape from the reactor.

control rod: A device constructed of neutron-absorbing material that is used to regulate a chain reaction by its placement within a reactor core.

core: The region of a nuclear reactor that contains the nuclear fuel.

decommission: To permanently shut down a nuclear power plant.

electron: A negatively charged particle that exists outside the nucleus of an atom.

element: A substance that cannot be chemically separated into a simpler form.

fission: Splitting a nucleus of one atom, resulting in lighter nuclei of other atoms and the release of energy.

fuel assembly: A group of fuel bundles with a cavity in the center to contain a control rod.

fuel bundle: A cluster of sealed, metal tubes containing fuel pellets.

fuel pellet: The smallest component of manufactured nuclear fuel, the size of a pencil eraser.

fuel rod: A sealed metal tube inside which fuel pellets are stacked end to end.

generator: A machine that converts rotational mechanical energy into electrical energy.

heat exchanger: A device used to transfer the heat from one medium to another.

main power transformer: Increases the voltage from the generator to a level suitable for long-distance transmission.

meltdown: The melting of a portion of a reactor core caused by insufficient cooling of the fuel.

neutron: A particle with no charge that is found in the nucleus of an atom, except for a hydrogen nucleus.

nucleus: The mass at the center of an atom consisting of protons and neutrons and having a positive charge.

pressure vessel: The strong container making up the exterior of a nuclear reactor that is designed to withstand the pressure and high temperatures associated with the fission process.

proton: A positively charged particle in the nucleus of an atom.

radiation: Energy emission in the form of particles or waves.

radioactivity: The property of certain elements that causes the emission of radiation resulting from spontaneous changes in the nuclei.

radon: A naturally occurring radioactive gas produced from the decay of radium in rock.

reactor: A device in which a nuclear fission chain reaction can be started, maintained, and controlled.

spent fuel pool: A repository at every nuclear power generating plant where used nuclear fuel is stored underwater.

steam generator: A heat exchanger in which the heat from the primary coolant loop is transferred through the walls of tubing to the secondary coolant loop, causing the water to boil, making steam.

terrorism: The use of violence and threats of violence to intimidate the opposition.

turbine: A machine with an internal rotor equipped with blades that is driven by steam to produce rotational mechanical energy to drive a generator.

yellowcake: Uranium oxide processed from uranium ore and used as the raw material for nuclear fuel.

For Further Reading

Michael J. Daley, *Nuclear Power: Promise or Peril?* Minneapolis: Lerner, 1997. Explores opposing viewpoints on nuclear power, especially those involving safety, pollution, and waste.

Susie Derkins, *The Meltdown at Three Mile Island*. New York: Rosen, 2003. An overview of the nuclear power plant at Three Mile Island and the accident that took place there.

Paul Dowswell, *The Chernobyl Disaster: April 26, 1986.* New York: Raintree/Steck-Vaughn, 2004. A detailed look at the Chernobyl nuclear power plant accident.

John Giacobella, *Nuclear Power of the Future: New Ways of Turning Atoms into Energy.* New York: Rosen, 2003. Discusses the pros and cons of using nuclear energy to supply our electricity needs.

Mark Mayell, *Man-Made Disasters: Nuclear Accidents.* San Diego: Lucent Books, 2003. A look at some of the accidents that have taken place in nuclear plants and with nuclear weapons.

Josepha Sherman, *Nuclear Energy.* Mankato, MN: Capstone Press, 2004. Explains the history, uses, advantages, and disadvantages of nuclear power.

Charlotte Wilcox, *Powerhouse: Inside a Nuclear Power Plant.* Minneapolis: Lerner, 1996. A look at the construction of a nuclear power plant, illustrated with photographs.

WORKS CONSULTED

Books

Stephen E. Atkins, *Historical Encyclopedia of Atomic Energy*. Westport, CT: Greenwood Press, 2000. A comprehensive encyclopedia of everything relating to atomic energy.

Edison Electric Institute, *Nuclear Power: Answers to Your Questions*. Washington, DC: Edison Electric Institute, 1987. Answers to some of the most commonly asked questions about nuclear power.

Nuclear Energy Institute, *Guide to Nuclear Energy*. Washington, DC: Nuclear Energy Institute, 2001. An overview of nuclear power generation in the United States.

U.S. Nuclear Regulatory Commission, *Regulatory Guide 4.7: General Site Suitability Criteria for Nuclear Power Stations*. Washington, DC: Nuclear Regulatory Commission, 1998. The official NRC regulations for choosing a site for a nuclear power plant.

———, *Regulatory Guide 1.68: Initial Test Programs for Water-Cooled Nuclear Power Plants*. Washington, DC: Nuclear Regulatory Commission, 1978. The official NRC regulations for start-up testing of a nuclear power plant.

Jack H. Willenbrock, *Planning, Engineering, and Construction of Electrical Power Generation Facilities*. New York: John Wiley, 1980. A step-by-step look at the construction of nuclear and fossil fuel power plants.

Jack H. Willenbrock, ed., *Construction of Power Generation Facilities: Experience with the Implementation of Construction Practices, Codes, Standards and Regulations*. New York: American Society of Civil Engineers, 1982. Technical information on different aspects of power plant construction.

Periodical

Michael E. Long, "America's Nuclear Waste," *National Geographic*, July 2002.

Internet Sources

David Dinsmore Comey, "The Fire at Brown's Ferry Nuclear Power Station," Canadian Coalition for Nuclear Responsibility, 1976. www.ccnr.org/browns-ferry.html.

Larry Craig, "Craig Convenes Nuclear Meeting with Vice President and Energy Secretary," press release, October 2002. http://craig.senate.gov/releases/pr100802a.htm.

Dwight D. Eisenhower, "Atoms for Peace," United Nations General Assembly, 1953. www.iaea.or.at/worldatom/About/atoms.html.

Albert Gore, "The Lesson of Chernobyl," speech, July 1998. www.nei.org/doc.asp?docid=651.

Kathryn Jean Lopez, "Nuke Fears: The Truth Behind the Hype," *National Review Online*, October 2001. www.nationalreview.com/interrogatory/interrogatory102501.shtml.

Robert Martin, "The History of Nuclear Power Plant Safety," American Nuclear Society Public Information Committee, http://users/owt.com/smsrpm/nksafe/about.html.

———, "The History of Nuclear Power Plant Safety: The Fifties," American Nuclear Society Public Information Committee, http://users/owt.com/smsrpm/nksafe/fifties.html.

———, "The History of Nuclear Power Plant Safety: The Forties," American Nuclear Society Public Information Committee, http://users/owt.com/smsrpm/nksafe/forties.html.

Nuclear.com, "Diablo Canyon–NRC's Reply to Sen. Boxer's Post-Earthquake Request," www.nuclear.com/archive/2003/12/25/2003/225-001.html.

Nuclear Energy Institute, "Congress Approves Energy Appropriations Bill; Yucca Mountain and Nuclear R &; D Benefit," 2003. www.nei.org/doc.asp?catnum=2&catid=287&docid=&format.

———, "Nuclear Fuel Transportation Containers Tested for Safety." 2004. www.nei.org/index.asp?catnum=2&catid=81.

———, "Personnel Training," www.nei.org/doc. asp?canum=3&catid=47&docid=&format.

————, "Used Nuclear Fuel Shipments: Public Safe from Radiation," www.nei.org/doc.asp?catnum=2&catid=243.

Wolf Sterling, "The SL-1 Reactor," Radiationworks. www.radiationworks.com/sl1reactor.htm.

U.S. Department of Energy, Office of Nuclear Energy, Science and Technology, "Nuclear Power Systems: Nuclear Power 2010," www.ne.doe.gov/NucPwr2010/NucPwr 2010.html.

U.S. Nuclear Regulatory Commission, "Who We Are," 2003. www.nrc.gov/who-we-are.html.

World Energy Council/Conseil Mondial de L'Energie, *Energy for Tomorrow's World—Acting Now!*, 2000. www.nei.org/ doc.asp?catnum=2&catid=117.

Yankee Rowe Nuclear Power Station, "Decommissioning: Reactor Vessel Shipment," 1997. www.yankee.com/decommissioning_removal.html.

Web Sites

Control the Nuclear Power Plant (www.ida.liu.se/~her/npp/demo.html). A Web site sponsored by Linkoping University in Sweden, where one can virtually operate a nuclear power plant reactor.

Nuclear Energy Institute (www.nei.org). The institute's Web site is an excellent source of information on all aspects of nuclear power, including current data and news relating to the industry, as well as teacher and student sections.

Nuclear Regulatory Commission (www.nrc.gov). The Web site of the official government organization that oversees nuclear energy, with links to technical specifications and public relations information.

Nuclear Tourist (www.nucleartourist.com). A wealth of information about worldwide nuclear energy, as well as virtual tours of the world's nuclear power plants.

Radiationworks (www.radiationworks.com). A site with links to interesting aspects of nuclear power, such as the atomic airplane and the SL-1 reactor accident.

INDEX

PICTURE CREDITS

ABOUT THE AUTHORS

Marcia Lüsted has a degree in English and secondary education, and Greg Lüsted has spent over twenty years in the nuclear power industry. They live in Hancock, New Hampshire, with their three sons.

DATE DUE

DEC 0 1 2011			

HIGHSMITH 45230